The GATHERING

For

Anne Hirondelle
Claire Koenig
Lisa Muller
Marsha Rasmussen
Nancy Scott
Tree Swensen
Jan Thompson
Nirupa Umapathy

ISBN: 979-8-218-16149-1

GALEN GARWOOD is an American artist of various disciplines—painting, printmaking, photography, filmmaking, and writing. Born in Georgia in 1944, at 16, he migrated to Alaska and eventually settled in Seattle, Washington. He began his professional life as a painter in the early 1970s with Seattle's Foster/White Gallery. He has exhibited his paintings throughout the United States and Europe; his award-winning multi-media "Adagio" was included in the 1993 Venice Biennale's *Xenographia Nomadic Wall* and as part of Art Affair in New York, 1994. His film "Cadmium Red Light" received the First Place Award for Short Docs at the Port Townsend Film Festival, and his documentary "Ed and Ed" received First Place at the De Reel Film Festival, Victoria, Australia. He has collaborated with numerous poets and musicians, and he published his memoir *Sell The Monkey* in 2018 and a novella, *BENCH, A Story of Wonder* in 2022. He currently lives in Thailand, where he continues to make art.

Cover Image: detail from "The Crowd', oil on panel, 2015
Interior images by Galen Garwood

*"Ed and Ed" and "Kados and Me" appear in *Sell The Monkey, an Artist's Memoir, Second Edition* by Galen Garwood, Marrwstone Press, 2022

The GATHERING

A selection of Poems, Images and Ruminations

by
GALEN GARWOOD

MARROWSTONE PRESS   SEATTLE

CONTENTS

A Note from the Artist *i*

Poems

Eros

RUMINATIONS

A Note from the Artist

I am perpetually reminded of my age, not only by Kados, my beloved other self but by this river of time on which we have no choice but to sail, leaving ever-accumulating memories like dying red and ochre leaves gathering beneath the trees, becoming food for lives that follow.

Most of my productive adult years have been making visual art—paintings, monotypes, photographs/galenographs, mixed-medium, and later in life, video and film. In 1964, I transferred from the University of Georgia to the University of Alaska near Fairbanks. At the time, U of A didn't offer Art Majors, so I began with a Major in Music and Literature; a year later, when the University offered it, I was granted a Major in Art.

Here in this frozen land of long winter nights, I began to write my first poems. I studied under Edmond Skellings, who became the Poet Laureate of Florida from 1980-2012. Arriving from the University of Iowa, he began the Alaska Writer's Workshop in 1963 and founded The Flying Poets with Donald Kaufmann, Lawrence Wyatt, Kenneth Warfel, and Robert King. I took classes with most of these poets and writers during my three years there before eventually resettling in Seattle. In 1983, after twelve years in Seattle, I moved to Port Townsend, Washington, where I became friends with Sam Hamill, Tree Swenson, and William O'Daly, co-founders of Copper Canyon Press, notable for its publications of poetry; both Hamill and O'Daly are remarkable poets and translators of poetry, and Swensen brought her exceptional ideas and book designs. Between 1983 and 1998, I was lifted and widened by such creative minds; through them, I became friends with many poets: Marvin Bell, Denise Levertov, Hayden Carruth, Peter Weltner, Carolyn Kizer, James Broughton, and others.

This book is a gathering of my few poems written over the years, with selected images, primarily photographs or monoprints, that reproduce better in black and white, and a few essays reflecting my viewpoints on everything from elephants to homosexuality.

The impetus to gather these various expressions I owe to my cat. Let me explain. I'm not a cat person—never have been. And no one in my immediate family kept a cat or any pets I can recall, except my mother's three poodles, two monkeys, and Queenie, the pig. Not until I was in my early twenties did I have my first cat encounter. One of my college room-mates had a cat in our shared house near campus. I never paid any attention to it until one night, when everyone was elsewhere, and I was alone, sitting in the living room's big chair reading a book, I felt the presence of someone watching me.

I looked up and saw the cat sitting in the doorway, intensely staring at me. I went back to my reading, but peripherally I could track the cat slowly moving toward me, then sitting at my feet, looking up, its bottomless eyes swallowing the light. Why she seemed so darkly focused on me, I have no idea. Was I the enemy? Dinner? Foolish thoughts. I tried regathering my attention, climbing back into the book's story. Impossible; I felt increasingly anxious from this intimidating feline forcefield intruding into my space.

Suddenly, like a bullet, the cat shot from the floor onto my chest, her face pushed into mine, eye to eye. I dropped the book and froze, fearing her claws would rip into the flesh of my neck. After a ten-second faceoff, the cat retreated as quietly as it had appeared, slipping back into wherever she had come from. What was the cat up to? Was she trying to relay some cosmic message or simply having fun? In any case, I closed the book, turned off the lamp, and slid into the safety of my bedroom. Good night. So, no. I'm not a cat person.

However, forty years later, living in another country, a nearby friend called me one day for a favor. Some cruel human had disposed of an unwanted two-week-old kitten, tossing him into my friend's fenced yard, and since Peter already had three cats, would I please adopt this adorable black furry male creature, desperately needing love and affection. Foolishly, not only did I not say no, an affliction I'm well aware of, but within a week, I adopted another male kitten, white with grey spots, thinking the two would enjoy growing up together.

I soon moved from the city to the countryside into a house I built by a narrow river, and the cats easily and quickly adjusted to their new boundaries. At first, the kittens were the same, except for their coloration. As they got older, the similarities diminished until they were, in fact, as different as black and white. Despite the trauma the black cat had suffered in his first few weeks of life, he was gentle and loving, grateful for the attention and never crying to be fed, obviously gifted with natural homeostasis. However, after a year, for some reason, the black cat, who I'd named Sīdåm, the Thai word for black, decided to go live elsewhere, either moving in with a nearby household or preferring to live in the woods, alone, away from its adopted brother, Sī khāw (white) who was not at all loving nor did I find Sī khāw lovable. I'm aware cats generally assume a high degree of entitlement, befitting royalty, but S̄ī k̄hāw redefined the definition. He rarely purred or rubbed up against my legs and exhibited a degree of laziness even most cats would be ashamed of.

I would have preferred the long-tailed black cat stay and the white tailless cat disappear, but we're not in charge of such things. Because I had made that early decision to adopt them, I accepted the fate I was now charged with and fulfilled my duties. I fed the cat, gave him water, and occasionally talked to him, albeit not always so kind, but often enough, a pleasurable discourse between two different species unfolded. As the years went by, simply because of his genetic wiring, size, the earth's turning with gravity's inclination, and possibly his irascible attitude, the cat, which was already 24 years old two years after I adopted him as a newborn kitten, 56 years old by the time I was 72, and pushing 80 as I ventured toward my 78th year, began his decline. There was a general slowing down, more prolonged states of meditating, no doubt, on his early life in ancient Egypt, festooned in golden necklaces, dining on raw fish, treated as a god by his adoring family, and wondering why things cannot be the same now as then.

S̄ī k̄hāw became increasingly particular about what he ate...or what I fed him, consuming less and less until finally, the cat quit eating altogether, quickly losing weight. Within a week, he was all but skin and bones, growing weaker, listlessly seeking out dark, obscure places in the house, waiting, I suppose, for the end of the ninth. On his last day, I gently carried him outside. I looked into S̄ī k̄hāw's face, his eyes pleading for answers: What's happening? It seemed to ask.

I sat the cat down, and he immediately headed toward the river in front of my house. During his life, S̄ī k̄hāw never strayed too far and never went anywhere near the river, yet here he was, sitting and surmising the landscape, the far rice fields, and blue skies. Then slowly, awkwardly, he climbed down the small, steep concrete embankment to the water's edge, where he precariously meandered inches from the swift currents, struggling to keep his fragile skeleton from falling into the river. I watched and wondered if perhaps S̄ī k̄hāw would end it all then and there, a brave dive into an element that cats fear from birth. But he turned toward me with helplessness so intense I scrambled down, grabbed the cat, and brought him back inside the house.

Later that evening, as I climbed into bed, I was sure that night would be S̄ī k̄hāw's last. Sleep was difficult as I tossed beneath the covers, wondering about the threading together of two lives of two different species, realizing that so often, for so long, my attitude about S̄ī k̄hāw was more about me than the cat. How can it ever be otherwise?

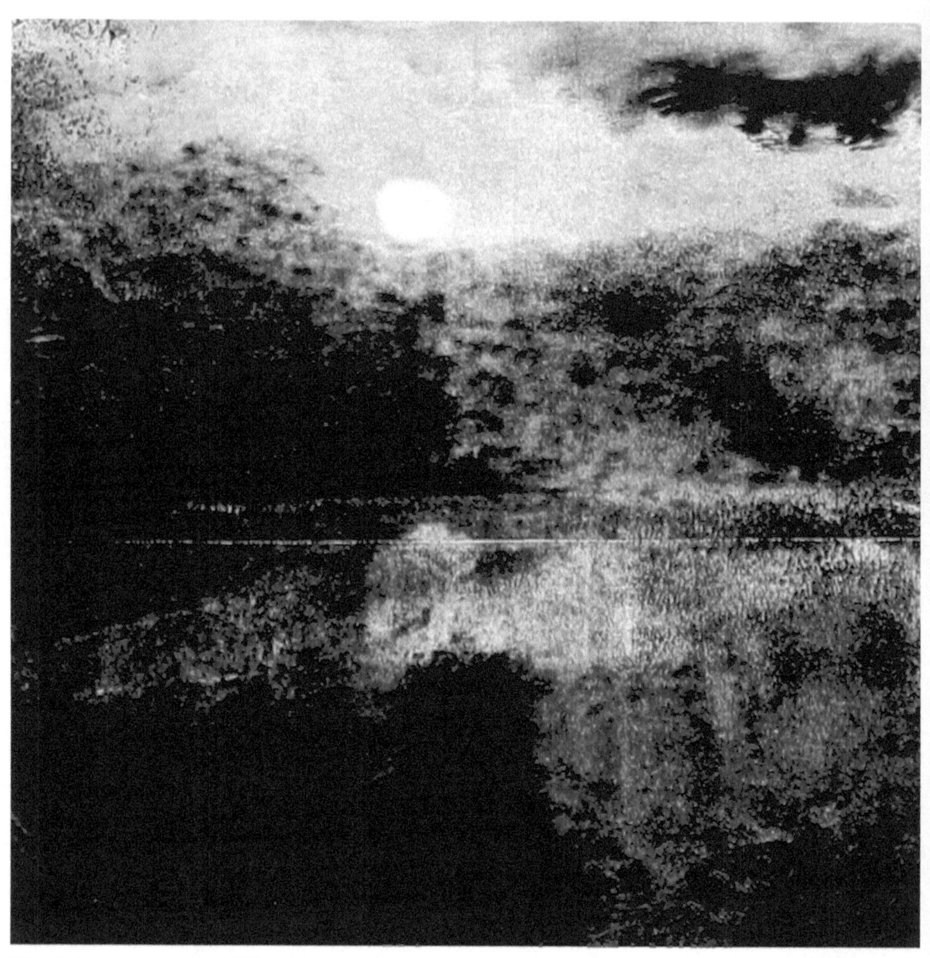

The Lake, monotype, ca 1995

I rose at first light, put the water on for my coffee, made my bed, and began looking for my four-legged housemate. I checked all the rooms. Nothing. I called his name. Nothing. I went to my office, sat in the leather chair, and turned on the computer. A feeling nudged in. I swiveled toward the wall behind me toward the bookshelf…and there was Sī khāw, lifeless on the bottom shelf in a small box containing printed copies of poems I'd written over the years. Rigor mortis had set in; the cat lay rigid as a statue, his eyes open as if waiting for me to say hello. As I picked him up, I saw that the top poem he died upon was face down, partially stained with residue from some universal life force leaking out and across the paper in the shape of a continent, a clue, perhaps, to the many 'whys' we're left with. An auspicious feeling washed over me as I gently lifted the cat from the paper and turned over the page, revealing 'The Fall of Clues,' a poem I wrote in the early 2000s. (page 72)

That evening, I buried Sī khāw beneath a large Jamjuri tree at the edge of the river, beneath a symphony of stars, their light timeless and irreducibly infinite.

There is no thematic or chronological order to the placement of these poems. These are the ones upon which the cat whispered its farewell.

I am a painter, a poet, a writer only insomuch as what I do, what I make, might help widen the wings of hope, these invocations that encircle me as I dive into the wordlessness of painting or to posit thoughts about this world, this singular reality that cradles me after all these years, here, with my most devoted companion and lover, Mystery.

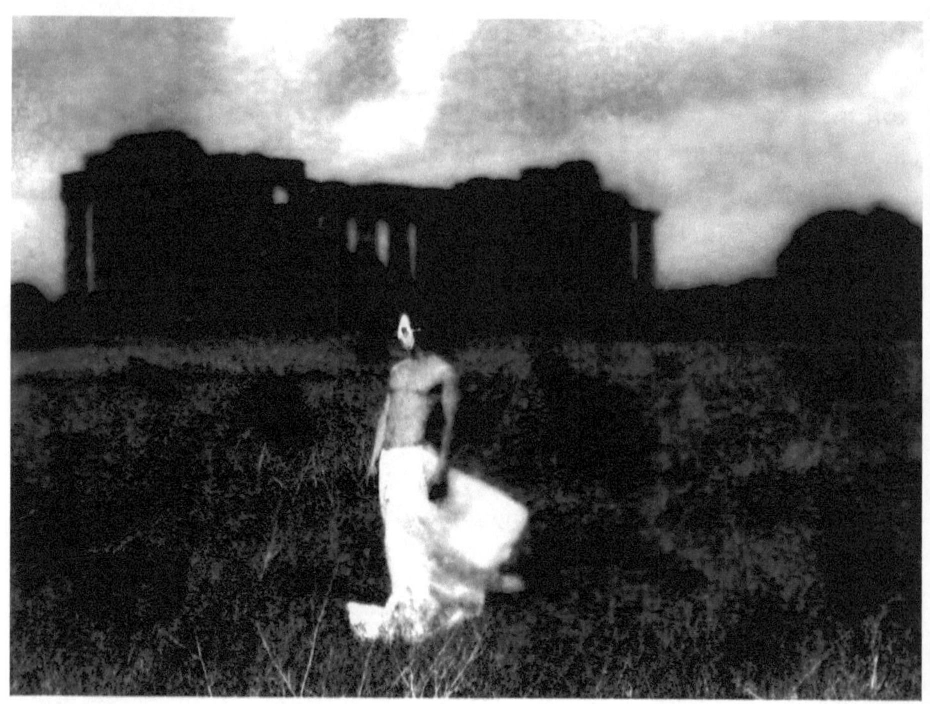

Temple Mask, Selinunte, Sicily 1996

THE BRIDGE

You will remember me
when this earth is no longer my home
but home for you.

You will remember me
while this notion of time
is carried on the winds

like the scent of orange blossoms.
We will never kiss,
nor caress.

We will never know the spaces
between us, nor cry
for the loss of things,

unable to measure such loss.
Yet you remember
the intoxicating touch of my lips.

You might imagine yourself a person of long ago.
I would make you so,
if I could.

White Peonies

What weight of beauty, she wonders,
will balance her life
within this room
where shadows fall
upon the vase in which the peonies bloom.

At the side of her bed she draws
in the table's dust a shape
the heart must take, leaving
a life's perfect turbulence
of light and dark.

Imprint

We are no more nor less the flower
   repeating itself,
      insisting to form,
a continuous touching, this cosmic lace,
   dancing through timeless space.

Unable to resist the changes
   or change the pattern of resistance,
      we are.

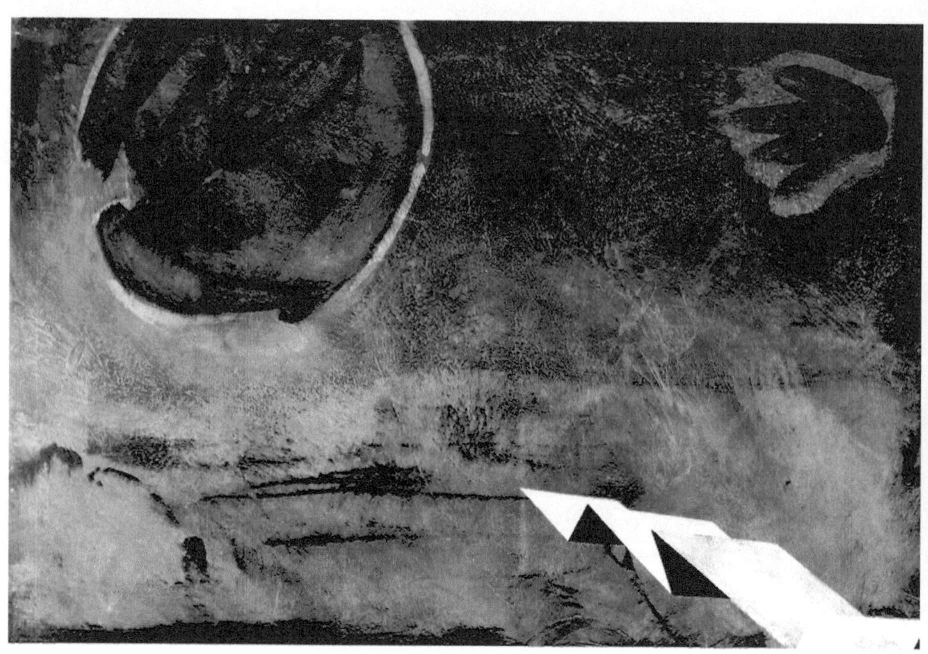

Reading the Seed, mixed-media on paper, 1995

Seed

for Marsha Rasmuseen

You are here.
Now.
Beginning the dream—
a slow fire unfolding
higher and higher.
All that breathes—
sky and earth, infinite song,
the suchness of your birth rising
toward blossom-dance, beautiful
artifact of soul
and circumstance.

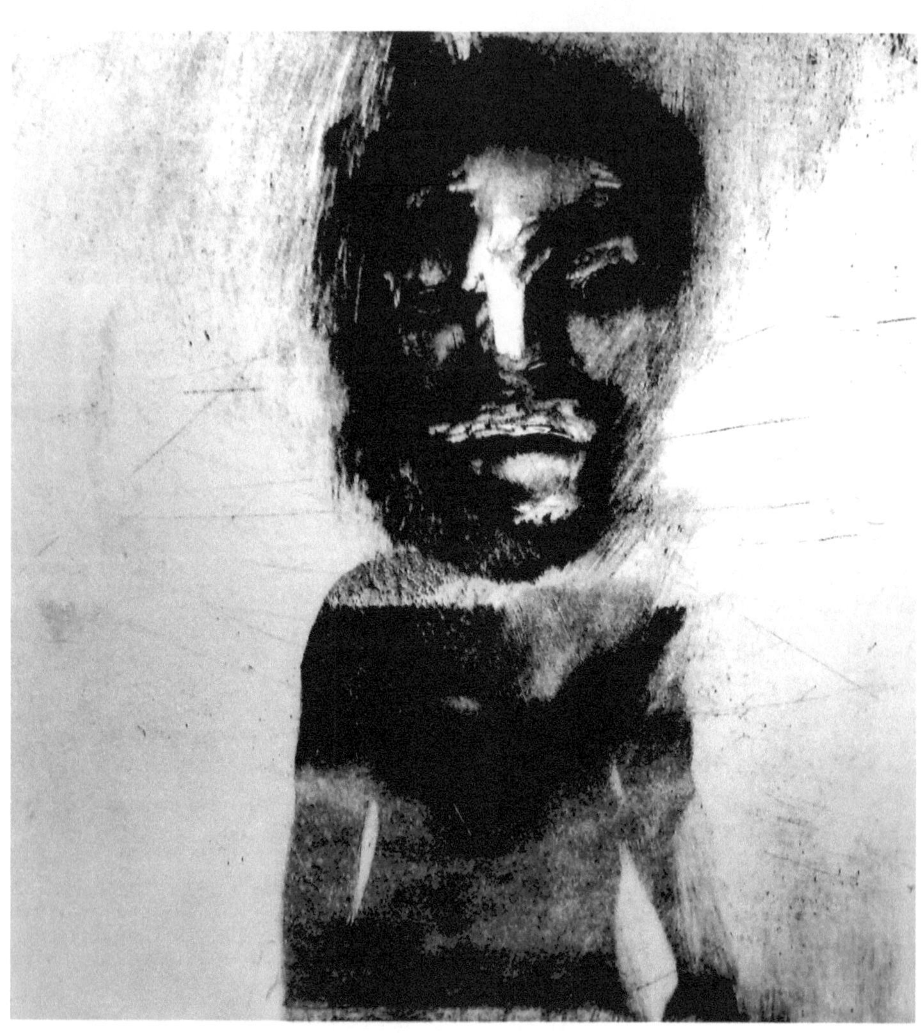

Mask of Chugos, monotype, ca 1994

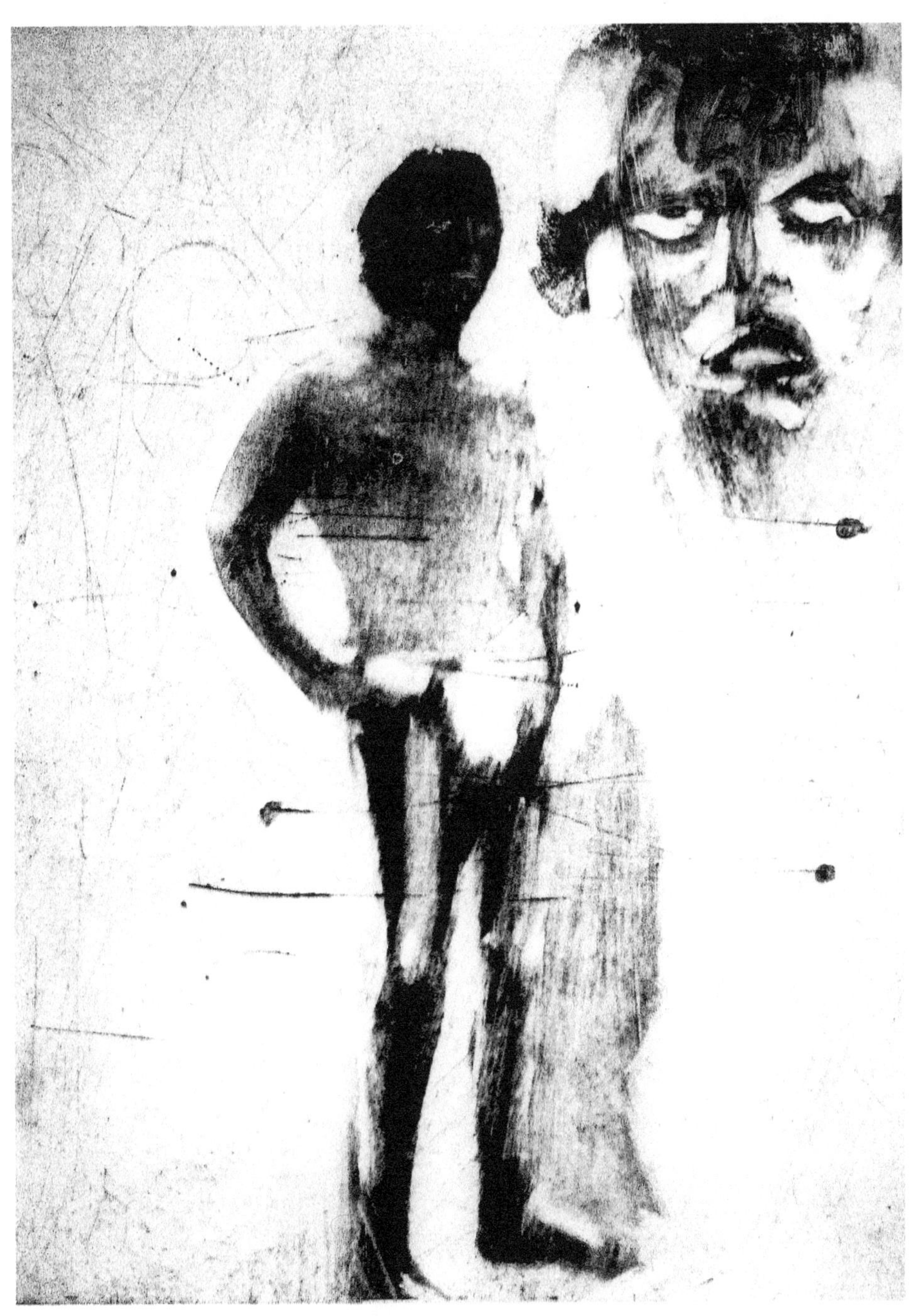

Waiting for Mammon, monotype, ca 1994

The Fox

A dark, dead thing, fallen into an apse
of blackness, frozen and thinly covered with snow,
lay upon a broken path from my home far below.
I knelt in silence to this sad collapse
of bones and fur, as if to prove a death by reverence.
I listened for that eternal song, a breathing
that lingers long after something greater
than hunger moves us.
She'd come far with one leg severed
still in the trap's deadly embrace, her blood red
against the white.
—Courage of the heart,
that fearless, insatiable fight for freedom—
We would do well to stop and pray
we too will know the difference and sing of it.

The Tree

is full of words, its limbs
heavy with meaning
and misunderstanding.
       The wind is full of noise.
Above it all, a solitary bird weaves
dead grass
in the eyes of the snake.

Maenam

All afternoon heavy clouds float
beyond grey mountains.
Rain tonight and rain
tomorrow.

The river takes and leaves
what she will. Fish and bird
marry the wind,
my heart clings to the lamp

A Thousand Trees

The Buddha gatheres the shadows
from a thousand trees and draws a line
between sky and sea. Then,
with the light of the lotus, Buddha touches
everything between mind and stars.
"When you come to the middle," he said,
you will find yourself."

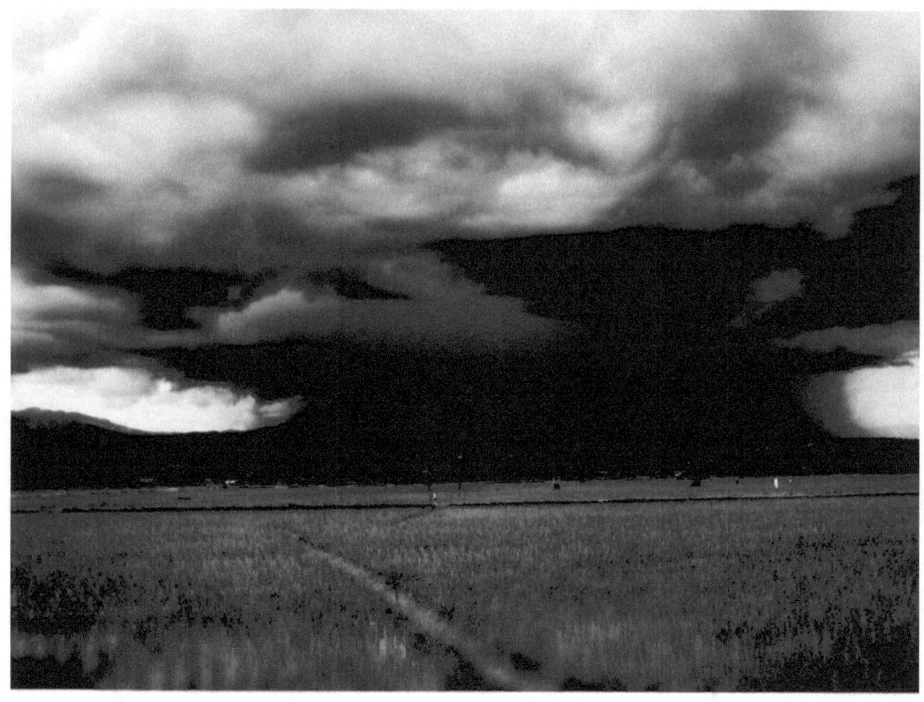

The Storm's Arrival, photograph, Chiangmai, Thailand 2011

Storm

It is the sky.
No, it is the light.
No, not the light, but the heat
that swims outside
within the light.

On the table below the window
lives a bowl of dying fruit,
and beyond, clouds scumble the horizon.
I wait in the dark silence of the room for rain
and the cool, electric smell of the storm.

Three Turns

December clouds hold us
close to the sleeping light of winter.

I'm touching all the parts
of your body with words.

The winds remember everything
in this beautiful snow.

Winter Dance

The creek is full of snow.
Everything, even the sound
of your name, lies suspended
in the blue ice of night.

When I reach to touch you,
You're not there.
You've gone dancing with the stars,
and water,
and moonlight.

Cobalt Blue

The disciple laid a wreath of purple flowers
at the Master's feet, then quietly
gathered up the dying lamps.

The hare sits frozen by the moon's trick, a voice
as thick as an icy river, heavy snow
breaking limbs of trees.

The snake burrows deep into the earth, her mouth
a cavern of colbalt blue night.
She listens for anything that moves.

Seed of Impermanence

The white lotus is dying, dark with decay.
The Buddha is dead.

Runnels of sorrow
flood the valley.

The river flows red, black clouds
thick beneath yellow skies.

Buddha's laughter claps like thunder
in dying light.

The Chair

There's not an empty chair in the room.
Stacks of books, piles of clothes, things
never used lay everywhere.
Your back seems unfamiliar now. Cold and brittle,
so tense even the dishes could cry.

Listen. I want to tell you things that'll make
a difference in our lives, but you're busy
fingering books, dividing yours from mine.
The paintings I gave you are good ones. Take them,
and take all the photographs too.

Promises we made last week, we might as well leave those
with the chair; it stays.
You stare across the room as if waiting for the door to speak.
It won't. What little to be said has been said,
while everything outside sweeps us apart.

I know you won't believe it, but the distances
we drift need not be so final. We need not carve
such indelible pain
in the folds of our heart where what is lasting grew
from the pulses of two people.

Let's pretend this chair that stays cares,
its arms weeping for the loss of things;
    of books and clothes that remember.

Let's pretend the chair wants to rehang the paintings.
Not exactly in the same place, but here,
    in this house,
with the books back, the clothes hung,
and the dishes dry.

Let's pretend for a while.
Let's comfort the chair,
    you and I.

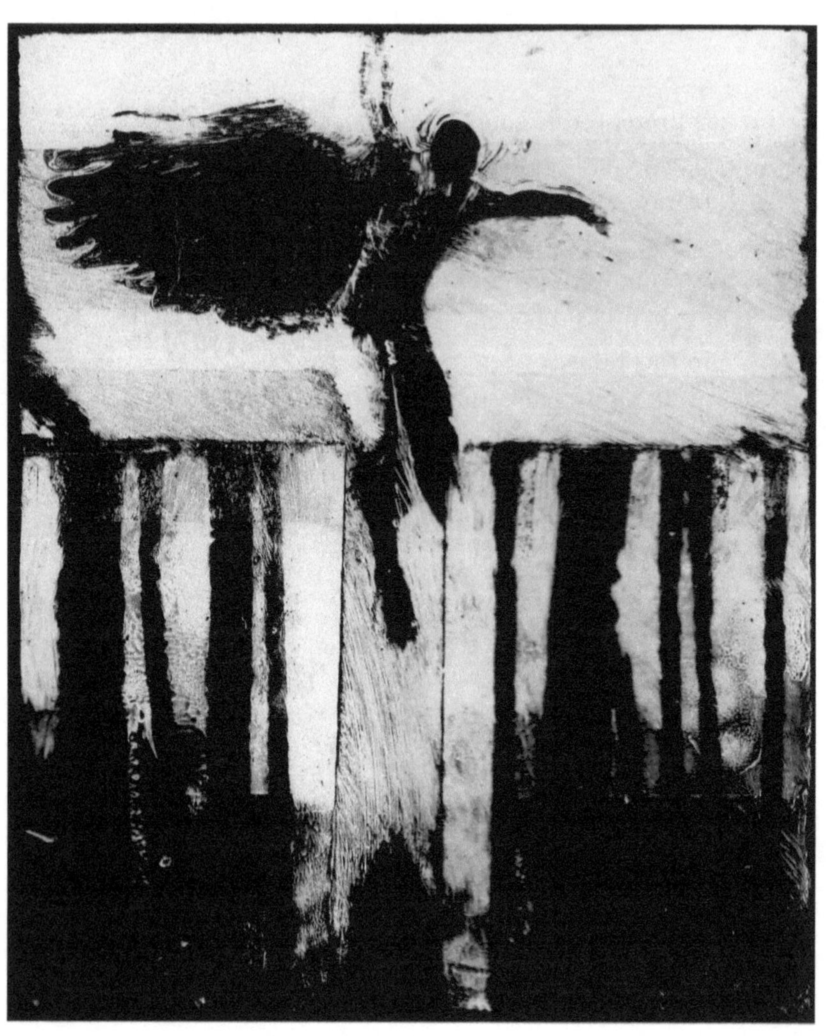

Hermes Rising, from PASSPORT, oil on plexi, 1984

Sic Eunt fata Hominum

Two dark birds storm the sky, each
moving the other in endless hunger, wings
hugging hearts, beating away the cold.

One bird bends
beneath the shadow of the other,
startled in its poverty of flight,

their cries lost in the wind.
But on they go, praying for gain,
that everything is theirs.

The Circle

for Nancy Scott

We've come along this circle,
turning, as circles do,
from the beginning,
turning,
now and then, as we must,
to the wisdom of this sphere, to the bright,
curious curves spinning out a life of clues,
year after year.
Let's dwell upon all we've seen,
what we've made of this earth
we call home and bow to those
who grew this place a little brighter—
a mystery, turning in the darkest night,
from which we all took flight.

Vessel

for Anne Hirondelle

Up from mud or such, turning
from the ground
with as much grace
    as air, as much
a song, your shape, your round form rising
up from nowhere,
a heartbeat coiled,
tenuous throated vessel, you
are made in the mind and palm
between memory and space,
earth,
and fire.

Someday

> *for Vincent*

There is, of course, the hue, I said
and of the hue,
should it be warm? Red?
Burnt Sienna?

It is blood, he cautioned,
sun and earth.
But you'll also need
what is cool—green to blue to black,
like strata of the sea.

We were standing near the edge of a spent field of grain
that fell to the sun and a raking mistral.
I brought only questions, I said, as he turned to his work
with a stony silence, chewing on the stem of a cold, blue pipe,
facing the wind, the fierce slapping of canvas, waiting
for imagination's raw nerve to let go a vision.

There is intensity, I said, and purity.
How deep the shade? How bright?
how much white? Should I
consider the opacity
and the amount of light let through?
Should it recede or dominate?

Remember, he said, within the color, there is the passage.
You might expect it to end all at once,
but it doesn't. It often wants to modulate
from subtle to bold, from hot to cold.

Yes, but will the hue be held by line? And the line,
will it be long or short? Thick or thin?
How should it be broken?
Or should it? Should it be continuous, holding

everything in?
Should it be dark or light? What value
and should it shift?
What weight?

Check for sincerity, he barked.
Lines can lie. Remember
there are timid ones, as well,
with low, slow curves that drift
unattached. Consider this: every line
has a beginning and an end.
Where does it start? Where
and how far will you take it?
It might only be implied.

I continued.
What about chiaroscuro?
and sfumato?
How deep?
Chould it be rendered a paraclete of lost beauty?
A palimpsest, perhaps?

Consider this, he said,
it's true; beneath the surface lies
another surface. But how many
must you uncover to find what you need?

I haven't yet thought that far, I said,
but what about shape?
And size? One large with many small?
Amorphous? Perhaps it would be nice
to have them all angular,
sharply defined. The shapes
will have to get to know each other.
Will they fight or make love?

He turned back into the wind. I could tell
by the movement of his ears he was smiling.
What about surface? I asked.
Texture. Should it be real or trompe l'oeil?
Should it dance with a scumble
or a stipple? How clear should it be?
How muddy? What of the sheen?
Should light slide across infinitely?

He bent to the earth
and scooped up a handful of dirt.
I suppose matte would do, he said, scrubbing out
an unwanted passage.
He turned to me, away from the wind.
Everything often dies on the borders, he said.
That's where you find the mood.
The pleasure.
The affliction.
Do you want it cosmic and reverential?
A mysterious essence moving into the center of things?
Something absurdly abstract? Or a political,
social implication, scratched then smeared in blood-red?
Profane deprecation?
A blind gesture?
Death?

What about a simple landscape, I said,
or a Chinese vase filled with peonies?
There is always the portrait. Always that.
I remember your Dr. Gachet's, his face filled
with what seemed wistful regret
beneath that ocher hat, his hands
painted a delicate flesh tint, his blue frock coat,
the yellow books on a red table,
the foxglove plant with purple flowers.

He looked up; a crescendo of wind-scattered clouds
and a rabble of crows sped across the burning fields,
a flash of black against the gold, against
the blue and white sky.

Someday, he said, pointing to the billowing canvas,
someone will look at this and find themselves amazed
to know they were here, in this stand of ragged wheat,
with all these hungry birds diving into the shadows,
you with all your questions, and me leaning into the wind.
This is where they'll find us...in this painting;
this is where we've always been.

Lunch with Monet

For John Franklin Koenig

Kreeee kreeee ka kreeee little unseen bird sings.
The valley dogs break into morning barks. I rise
and climb to my kitchen in the sky, dark still.

The moon
hangs over Mt. Suthep, then disappears into a flush
    of morning light.

Barefooted monks follow with empty bowls
the empty streets, the Buddha's promised path.
The day begins where nothing ends and ends
where everything begins.

The forest pond in the shadow of the temple
is hungry. The fish are hungry. The turtles are hungry.
The ducks circle in hunger.
    Leaves of the lotus arc to the east.

I'm not surprised to find you, John, in the cool depths,
treading among the tangled roots,
nor surprised to hear your voice.
Haven't we always been here?

you and I, arm in arm, gilding purpose
and promises of lunch with Monet,
his ancient knees
    collapsing.
The three of us laughing then crossing the narrow bridge
at the Gare d'Orsay.

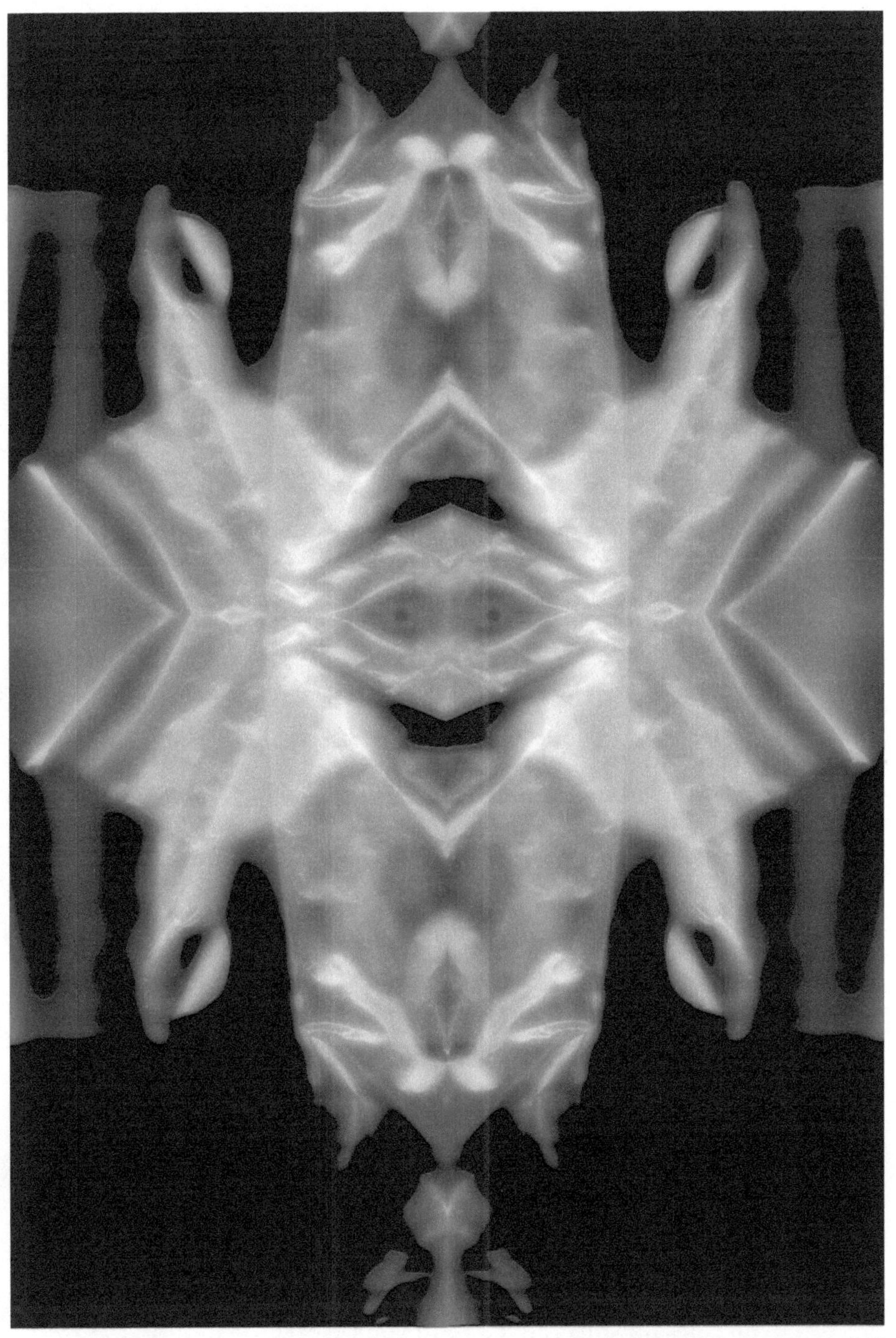

Ganymedes Mask, Phainomai 2007

A Letter to Alvin

for Alvin Neely, 1933-2022

Dear Alvin,
Well, here we are; you, spinning outward in exit',
and me, not too far behind.
We spoke only a few months ago about my next
visit, "You better hurry," were your last words.

Time is but a sea of memories—
first encounters,
the sharing of dreams, the pairing
of lives lived, the weighing of hopes
and what-ifs.

Remember the after-the-news sitting
on the screened back porch, twirling ice cubes
in our evening's first Negroni, listening
to the Kroger shopper shout across the darkening parking lot?
We laughed
at the world around us,
at ourselves, waiting
until the first of your guests arrived
within the soft illumination of lamps hovering
above the tables, the sofa, and chairs.
And you, dressed in your white polo shirt and khaki trousers,
sitting in your rocker,
your noble Ciceronian brow unfurling a quiet solicitude,
seduced us into a state of tranquility and laughter.
A joyful, mischievous reflection in your eyes
held us lovingly in that room,
in that house,
in that timeless space.

Everything you were still is. Everything that is
will always be. Here,
now, in this infinite sphere of possibility,
there's no need to hurry, is there?
No, none at all.

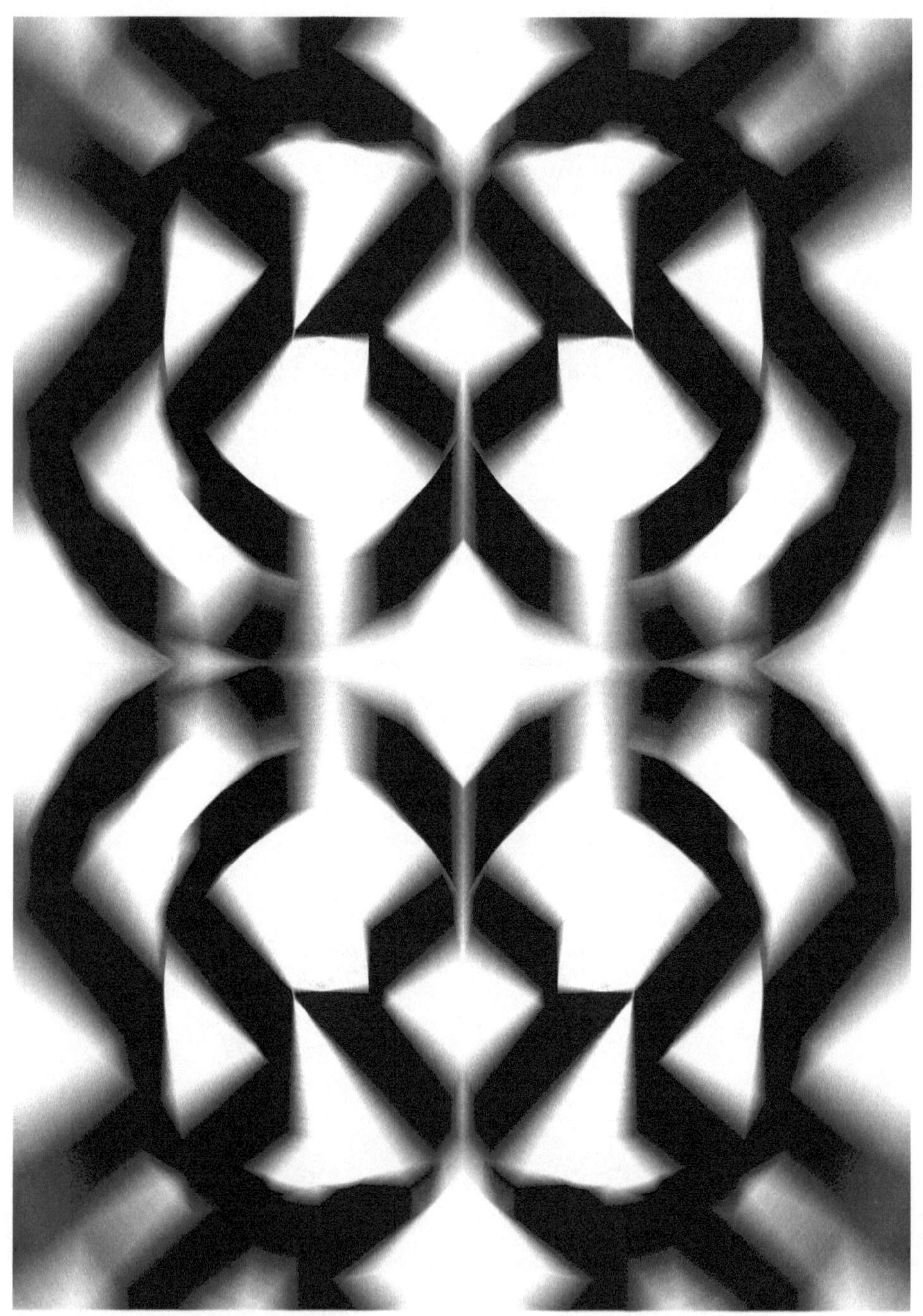

Take It As You See It, galenograph, 2022

Adam's Cradle

There was time
when hands would speak and cradle
our thoughts, palming
each moment
with quick bending of knuckles.

Long ago there was a time
when hands would speak—
not just for pushing away
or pulling close,
not just to point.

There was a time when what hands would say
would tear away any thought of time
before the shape of history fell dark upon the brow,
before the marriage of meaning
and voice took flight.

There was this time of night
when the heart and the heart's choice
was made with blood and hands held
within the pulse of our being
and our beastliness.

Tree

for Tree Swensen

In

reading

we read. In sowing we sow.

Though what is believed through reading

is not always what is sown, nor meant to grow, and so

it seems that planted seeds of thought are blown across the plains

of the mind. Reaping what we sow, we find the shape of life in lines of fer-

tile words, a sky, a whiter snow, home for birds, and blooming ideas, free,

and growing

out of you

and me

and this

read-

able

tree.

Butterflies

From a cloudless winter sky, a symphony of butterflies
descends into an undulating sea, their wings
dissolving into a future we'll never know,
navigating a singular purpose: this song,
this sacred passage: We come and we go.

Coming Down the Mountain

for Svare and Jeanne Forsland

There's no one to tell us when the cup is full
you said, as we came down the mountain,
scattering rocks and pebbles,

the curious birds and our own shadows
rolling before us
without a thought of consequence.

It is good, you said, to laugh with the gods,
to pray for a moderate cup.
It's the right ballast for the soul.

We can speak of flight, yes,
but gravity will always take us to the sea.
And if we measure friendship

with the brightness of our journey,
it won't matter what distance the stars
or how we gather their winter light.

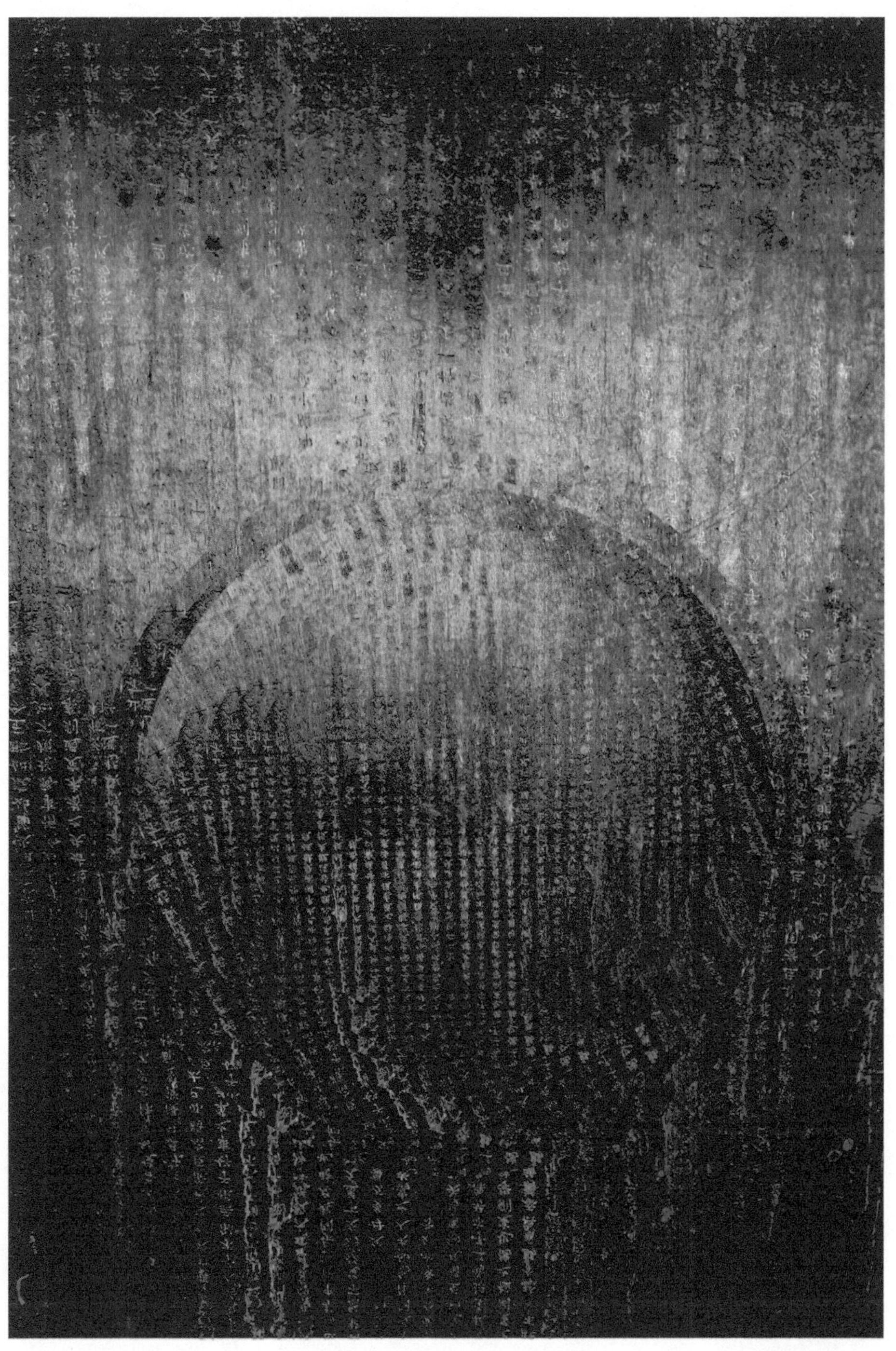

Mandala Vichara, Mandala Series, galenograph, 2009

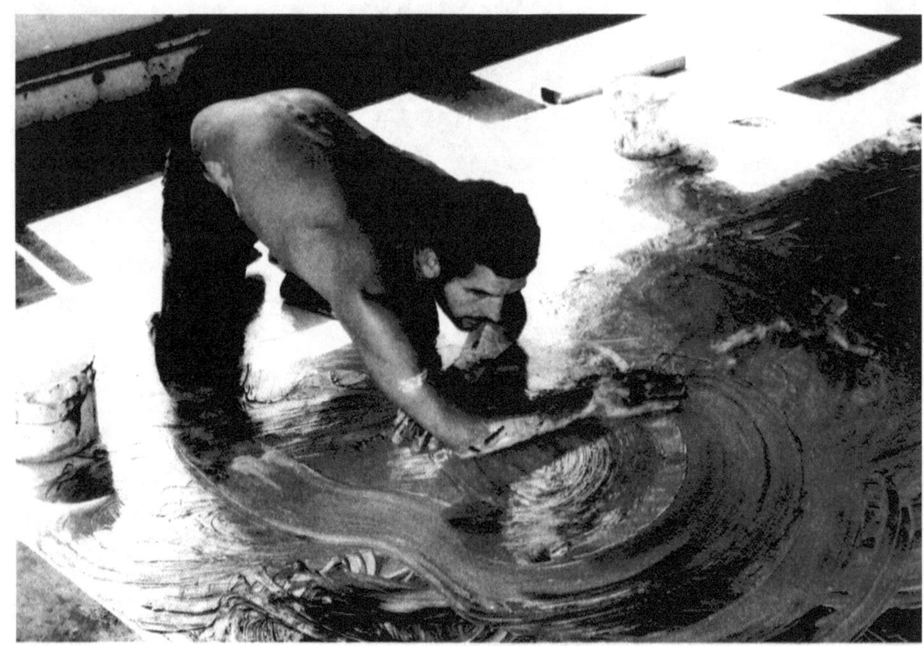

Portrait of the Artist, photographer unknown, ca 1981

Another Dream,

for Morris Graves

In a wreath of brightness, you've come astride in
your chariot of penetrating angles,
your irreducible world paired
with nothing more than lightness of air,
the deft scumbling of grey and ochre hues—
soft bruises—and the birds,
everything tumbling into this caldron of space.

Ravenous Blue

for Lisa Muller

On the far side of the rice fields,
beyond the Banyan tree,
an ancient carving of Buddha smiles, cradled
in rivulets of roots; still further,
beyond a narrow impenetrable wall
of green bamboo, she spied an out-of-place blue,
fluttering in dark shadows, sparking

memories from childhood—the wrapping
of a birthday gift or its ribbons—
a blue crying for attention with tangible intensity,
stark and ravenous,
demanding to be held in the mind
until all her reds and yellows
fall into greys and diminished umbers.

How can such a blue be so greedy, she wonders,
so unbelievably there? And where in her heart
can she possibly keep this unbridled hue?
when every color cries out to her
in a symphony of hope,
demanding a promise—
keep us safe, loved, and true.

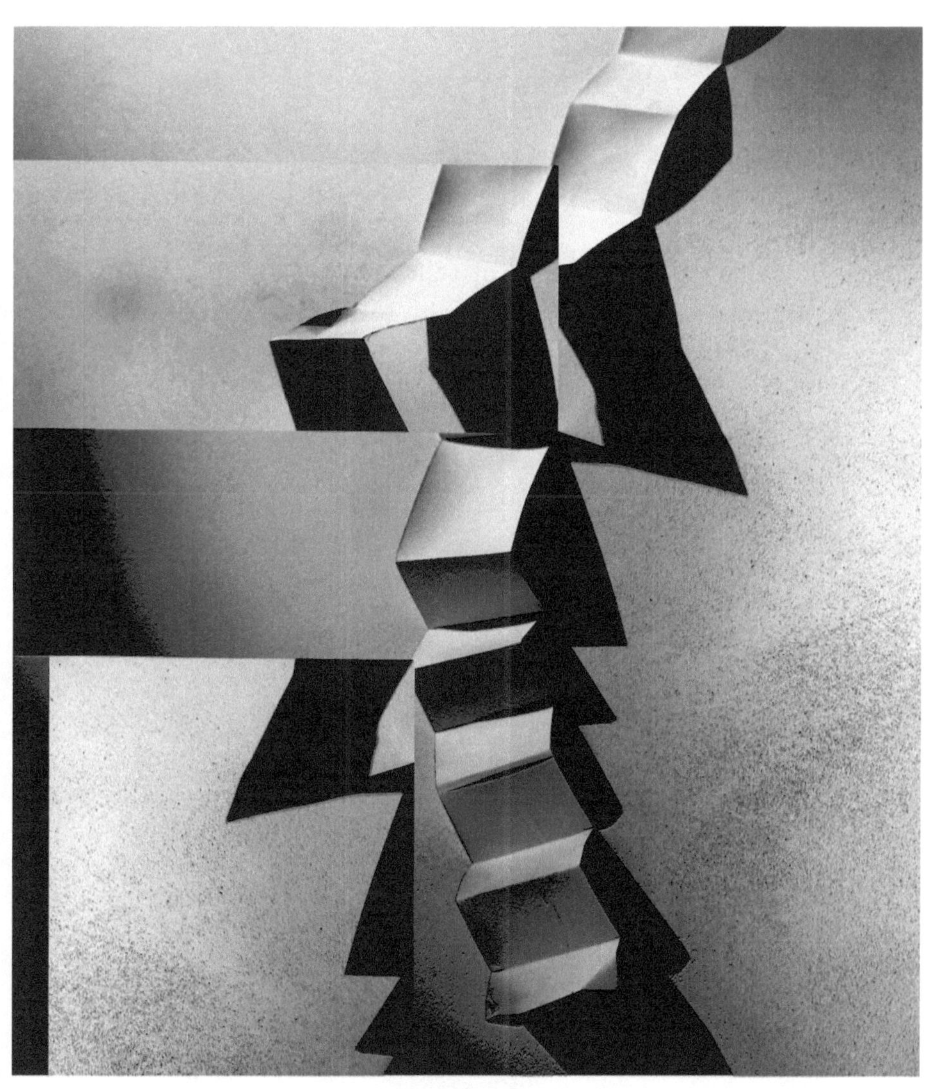

Empty Stairs Beneath the Stars, galenograph, 2022

Pigment

We define as much by what is not
as what is.

'What is yellow?'
and 'what is the meaning of yellow?'
are questions suspended in flight, intractably
out of reach.

We cannot think upon the questions,
nor the color,
without touching something else. Something
we've tasted—Ripe fruit.

Or something wrested from the heart—sense of time,
the blue pulse of night. Color is more
than vibrations bending the lens of the eye,
more than mechanical refraction.

Some curious, marvelous invention was made as well—
blood, hunger, a red
stain on the rock,
blazing in the yellow sun.

Stain

In the King's palace, the lovely children,
dressed in colorful silk, their hair
braided and banded in gold and silver, sing
of the ancient, white elephant
wise and revered,
    the Buddha reincarnate.

While in the fields, the mahouts,
for production's sake, spike
bananas with amphetamines and feed them
    to the giant beasts.

Soon their tusks grow brittle and break.
Their hearts thicken and convulse, a great
hurt settles in their eyes
and dark runnels of tears stain the dust
on their beautiful feet.
    One more stain of human consumption.

Empty Brush

for Claire Koenig

When I was young,
I wanted to paint big
and I did.
The older I get,
the smaller I want to paint.
This morning I painted the sky
the size of my checkbook; tomorrow,
a dream on the wing of a fly.
Someday, someone might stop and ask,
"Isn't this the painter
who painted nothing?"

Dear Marvin

for Marvin Bell

I'm overwhelmed, under the gun,
overworked, and under fire. Marvin, do you
believe the good Bible is bad, that
God's always on top of all of us at the bottom?

Marvin, I'm overstretched, under the counter,
over-sexed, and underlaid. I'm stacking the bills
beneath the table; some will get paid now,
some later.

Marvin, do you believe God
will eat her children
just to stay
on top of things?

The clouds have landed, and I'm overwhelmed,
overworked, and under the gun.
Marvin, do you believe in floating?
Are we still having fun?

The Ballad Of Ida's Leg and Last Rag

for Ida

My mother lies withering in her St.Sebastian bed,
her tilted heart broken, her right leg
already dead, the blackened foot
turned toward the artic light, long bloomed southern
rose suffocating in the cold, cold night.
"Bring me my camera she said, I want to document this.
This foot, these dark toes. I want
my grandchildren see what happened to me
could happen to them, Lord knows, anymore,
It's not enough just to tell them stuff,
there's got to be a picture."
Then she turned and asked with a sad, stoic grin,

"Would you like my leg as a souvenir...to bronze and keep
your pennies in, or to keep ajar the door?"
I only smiled and held her hand for a while
before the pain became more than she could stand.
"Cut the goddamned thing off," she cired. "Cut it off!
it hurts unbearably so."
But before they could, of course, my mother, ascending
on both elbows had to know,
"Hey Doc," she cried, "Will I hear the big saw go buzz?"
He smiled and held her hand for awhile.
"No, Ida, I really don't so."

Well, Doc, "I gotta ask it. This leg you take,
will it have its own tiny casket?
A box tied with string? Or will you strike a match
and just burn the damn thing?
"You see, Doc, this leg of mine has been the vine
that ties me to sky and earth. What goes up

always comes down and anything worth anything
always comes back around wrapped in music.
"My left foot is the tapper of time. The one you wanna take
sustains the line. It makes the music flow
soft like a river. Then it takes away your breath,
as cool as a shiver. "OK, Doc, let's do it, let's get to it, but,
before you do, I'd surely like to jag one last rag-
time tune for you bone boys up in the cutting room."

My mother cries in her St.Sebastian bed.
Half of her lies legless, the rest of her half dead,
her eyes, her blues eyes blazing.
"Good God almighty! They took away my leg, but the pain remains
deep inside, down near the floor;
it still hurts unimaginably so."

I couldn't really smile.
But I held her hand for the longest while,
waiting for the rest of dear Ida to go.

The Glass Light of Intention

Much of what you've said lives or dies behind me,
with your own dark and light. The life we've lived
has been sharp and swift—unsheathed arrows, now strung
on this bitter moment. Your narrow head, a god's head,
keeps turning out a cold wind,
an avalanche of sighs.

Late afternoon surrounds us
and the dying yellow sun lingers in your eyes
where shadows of hope fall and decay
from the bruises of easy lies.

Lazy gestures, broken promises,
and unspoken accounts of meaning,
float between us
swollen with silence.

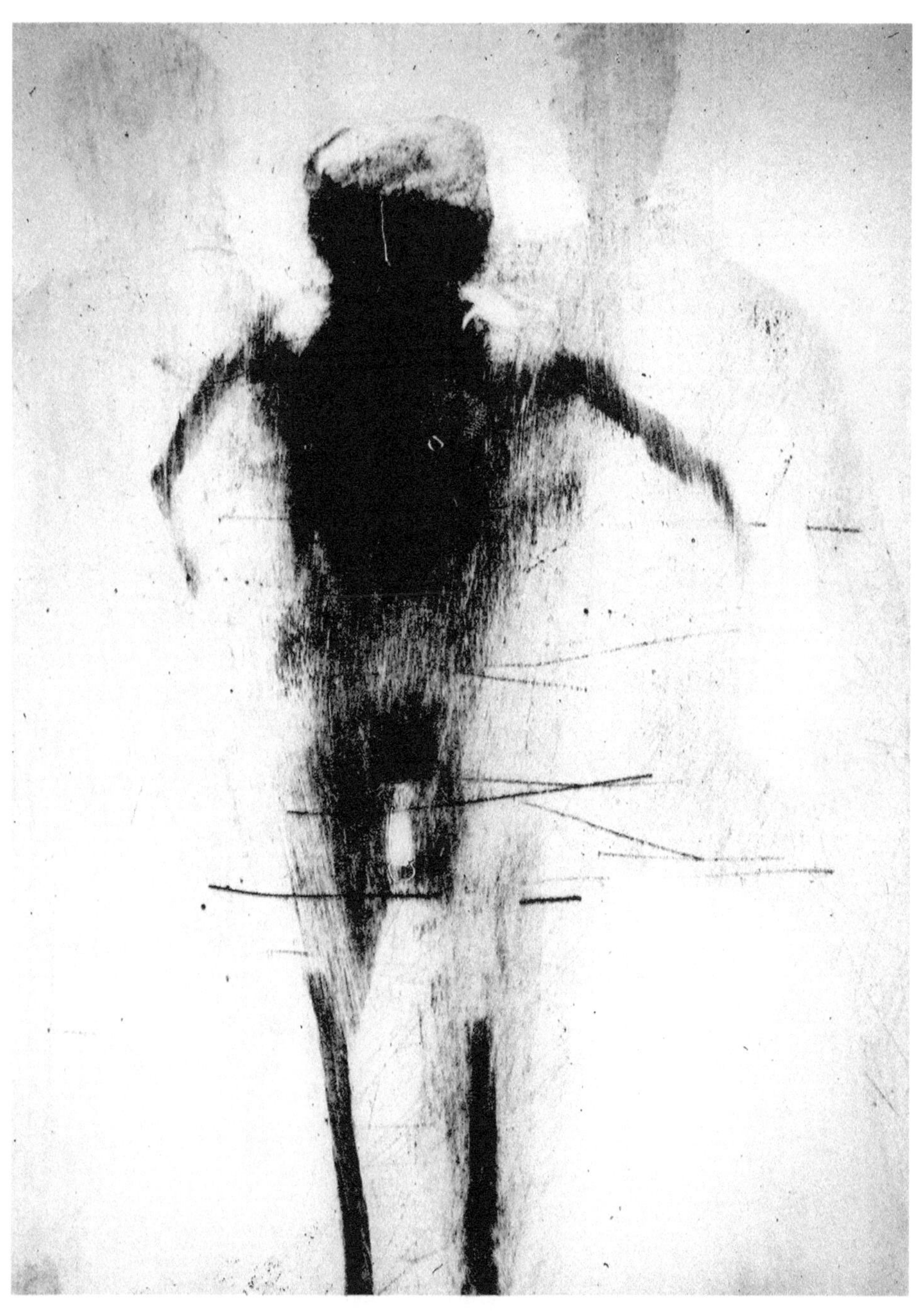

Three Figures, monotype, ca 1995

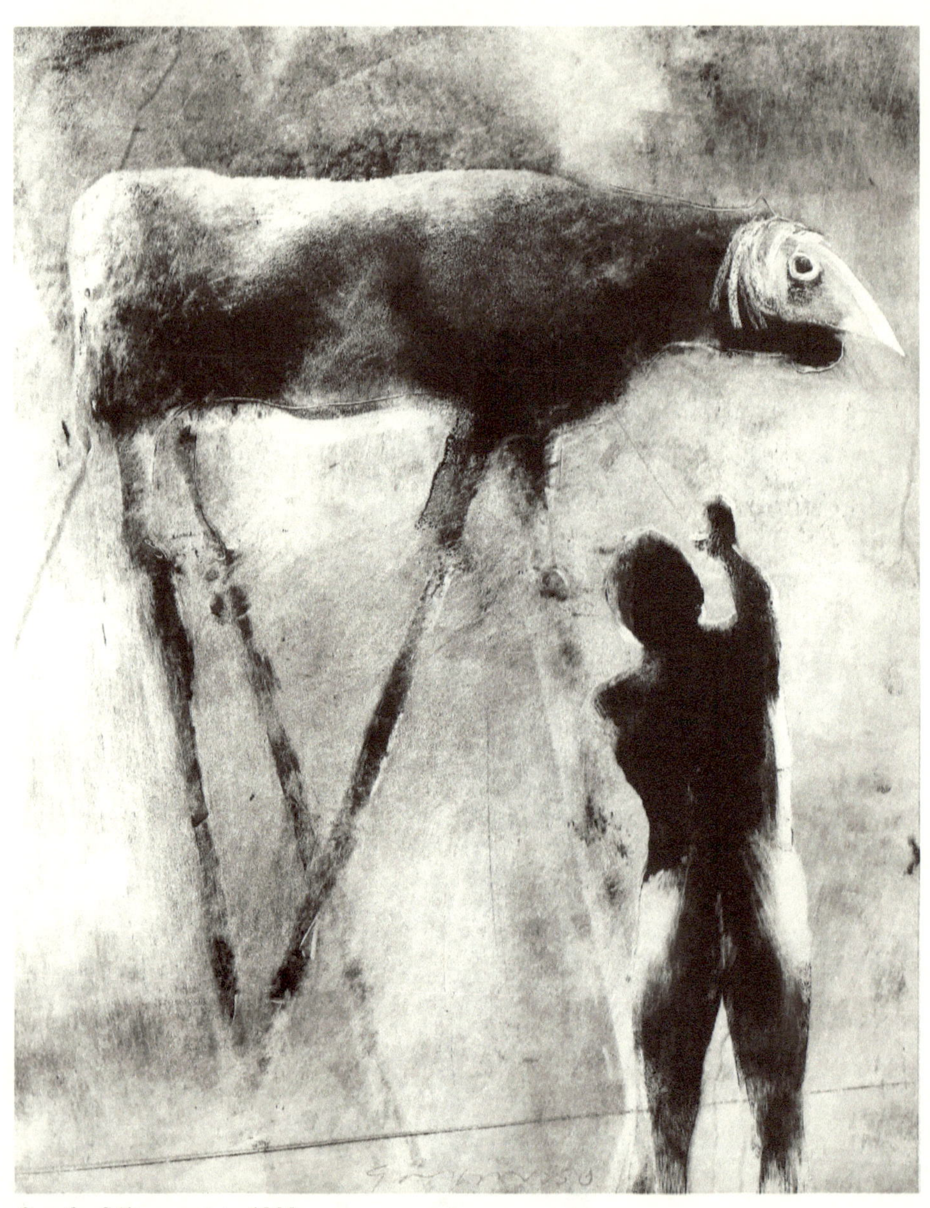

Cow On Stilts, monotype 1992

Cows in the Rain

For Hayden Carruth

Far down the highway, I saw through early morning mist
an object on the road, a mystery
until I was suddenly upon it.
I braked, approaching a silver car, askew on black asphalt.
Meadows of fallow land on either side, silent as the moon
disappearing into the distance.
A few hungry cows huddled nearby.

I sat startled, staring through the windshield,
waiting for movement or a sound.
Nothing. I stepped out and slowly approached the wreck
its front-end mangled, the engine still hot,
shards of glass cast like jewels across the road.
A dead boy, almost a man, lay crumpled and broken, his head
leaning into the steering wheel as if only sleeping.
The sun rose, and a gentle rain began to fall, darkening
his beautiful brown hair, as the cows belowed to the sky.

Floating Parable

Imagination
and Memory
have been lovers
it seems
forever.

The Garden

The room falls to inquiry.
The mind observes the sheer drop
of despair, a plummeting weight
of the heart,
gliding through
the autumn air among
the turning leaves of the garden, where
you once tended everything,
even the weeping of my soul.

Capsize

for Harold Glenn Garwood, 1941-2020

Brother, you and I were in the kitchen
making pineapple sandwiches for lunch.
You were seven.
I was four.
The lid to the jar of mayonnaise slipped
from my fingers
and fell to the floor spinning
in a lopsided dance till it quit, having landed
upside down. "Capsize," you said,
"That's what you call it
when something falls
and flips over onto the ground,
or when a boat is about to sink
into the sea."

The word burrowed into my brain,
where it waits, always, for the spiraling
sound of a fallen jar-lid spinning
onto the floor, that polished memory
breaking loose and rising still
with the winnowing song of your laughter,
a warm wind above my head.
You gave us something
in our trajectory of brotherhood, something dear
and enduring, two lost children surviving
an empty house, searching
for love, hope, and words,
the singing of the ocean
our only lullaby.

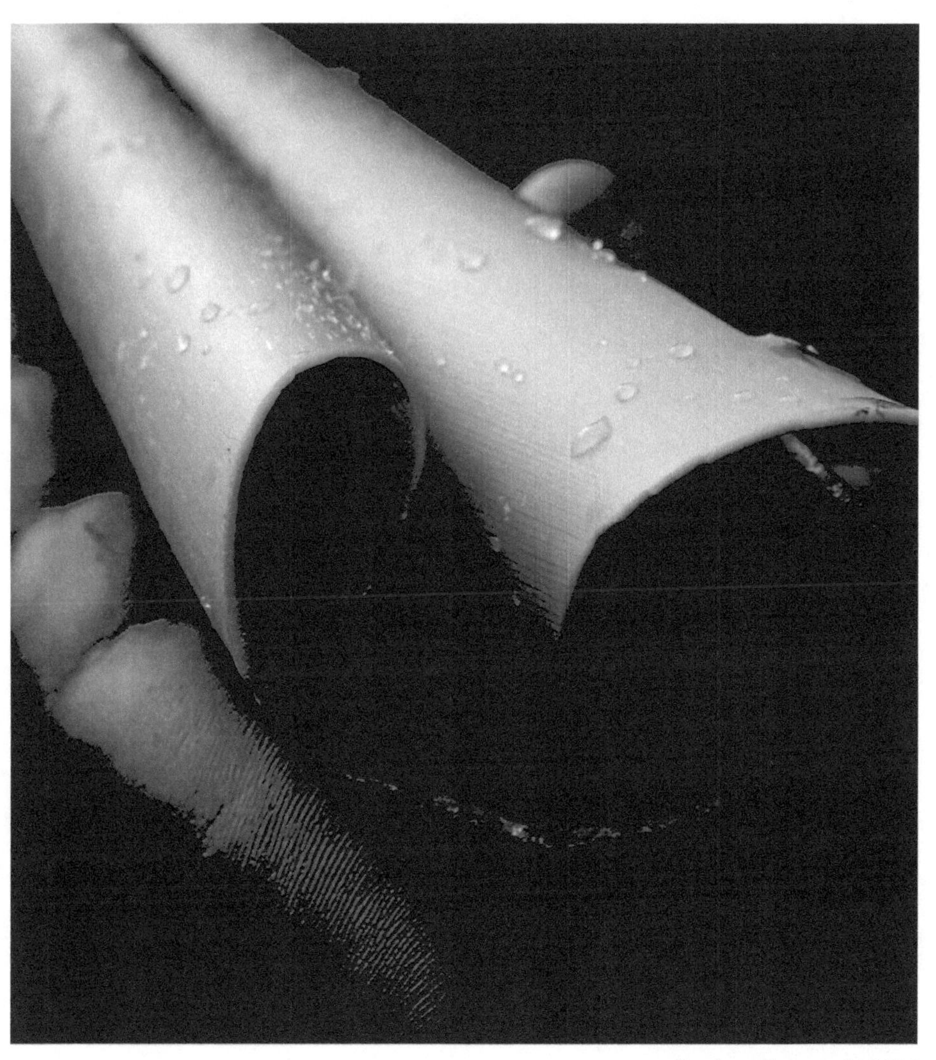

Bamboo, photograph, 2015

The Buddha with Six Toes

He stepped upon a soft pod and wrested
from the sweet mud of paradise
seven unanswerable questions:
Can we know from whence we come
and must always go?
Are we more than we are?
Are we less than we know?
Does time lead us back to the beginning?
Or do we take time to the end?
When is 'now?'
And when is 'then?'

The Riddle

Nine gods sat throned
in the middle of a riddle,
each desperate to win.

Nine times
nine clues rose
in nine different skins.

'Wise' is a word.
So is 'is,' as is 'a';
'word' too, by the way.

What is the riddle, then,
if it isn't you,
and everything you've wanted to say?

The Death of Peter Black

Elizabeth also buried the broken bottle
with which she cut her husband's throat.
It wasn't mean, she thought, to end it all, to bury him
with the marriage and the ring.
A broken heart's hunger turns the shovel easily enough
and every spade of dirt she put on him,
was a bruise he'd put between the sheets.

Kindness from men, she said, is like a whistle from a hen.
It rarely happens.
But when it did, she'd let him plow, just plow,
all goddamned night.
But no more, no more.
Her heart hasn't the hunger it had.
The eyes of hen she put in a blue bottle with a silver whistle, locked
in a box without a key.

Elizabeth hums a song her mother sang, and from the window
she watches the weeds grow.
For the life of me, she wonders,
why can't I remember his name?

Fairytale

The old men leave their homes in the early morning darkness.
They leave without permission, their families
deep in sleep. The old men slide
through the grey doors, all marching toward the street,
with only their nakedness and ancient bones,
full of memories,
full of brittle hope,
transparent with time,
full of petrified passion
and the dark perfume of age that settles,
year after year, from the heart
down to the feet.
The old men step into the cold dark air
and, one by one, they lay themselves down,
head to foot, together on the cold asphalt ground
and breathe as one.

Doubt

Lifted by a gentle wind, one pod of doubt
drifts above the land
then explodes upon an endless field of belief.

Its few urgent seeds
burrow into the soil
and soon, belief begins to crumble

from disease and chaotic furrows of discontent.
Such is the nature of humankind.
Such is the force of doubt.

Winter Solstice

There is an hour
appointed by the spinning suchness
of all of this,
when the trees' blood settles
about the stones and deepens
in sleep. If only we
could keep as still
and quiet.

Between Web and Star

for Nirupa Umapathy

A tawny spider fills her days on the ceiling of my kitchen.
She's been here so long I can't remember when she came; I'm not
even sure she's the same shy creature but in the evenings,
after I finish supper and tip the last sip of wine,
I acknowledge her presence, a toast to her being here,
her being so quiet in her observation of me in her world,
while I fill mine with noise and smells, clinks and clatter
from sink to stove to table.

We have no names for each other; that would only detract
from this silent communion. I'm grateful for her presence
and the simplicity of her life. Together, we help fill the world;
we do, we add something. She, far more patient than I,
spins and weaves a universe of waiting, without questions,
without recrimination.

Last evening, after supper, after finishing the last of the wine,
after measuring the distance between web and star,
here in the spider's presence and the rustling of her heart
as she moves the center of my universe to hers,
I thought, but for the size and density of duration, we are
immutably reflected in one flame, the same collision defines us,
again and again.

She'll be gone soon enough, leaving her brittle husk of fulfillment
collapsed in the tracks of the window sill among a multitude of legs
and spinnerets, beautiful debris of death dancing still.

Not knowing what more I could possibly say,
I offer these words, this poem, to fill our hearts
with what is left of our day.

The Gathering

Gather me up, bury me
beneath the trees, beneath
the red and ochre dying leaves. Bury me
below the roots, deep
in the soil of night, from which this flesh
and I took flight, this one continuous spiraling dream.
Bury this flesh, these bones beneath
embracing limbs of trees
into the sculpting hands of earth,
here, at the edge of light.

A Valentine's Poem

Curving
out of this blue sky, a red, so red,
a redbird's flight across the white
expanse of snow, so white against the heart,
this heart that bled a life, then died
and died so many loves ago.

EROS

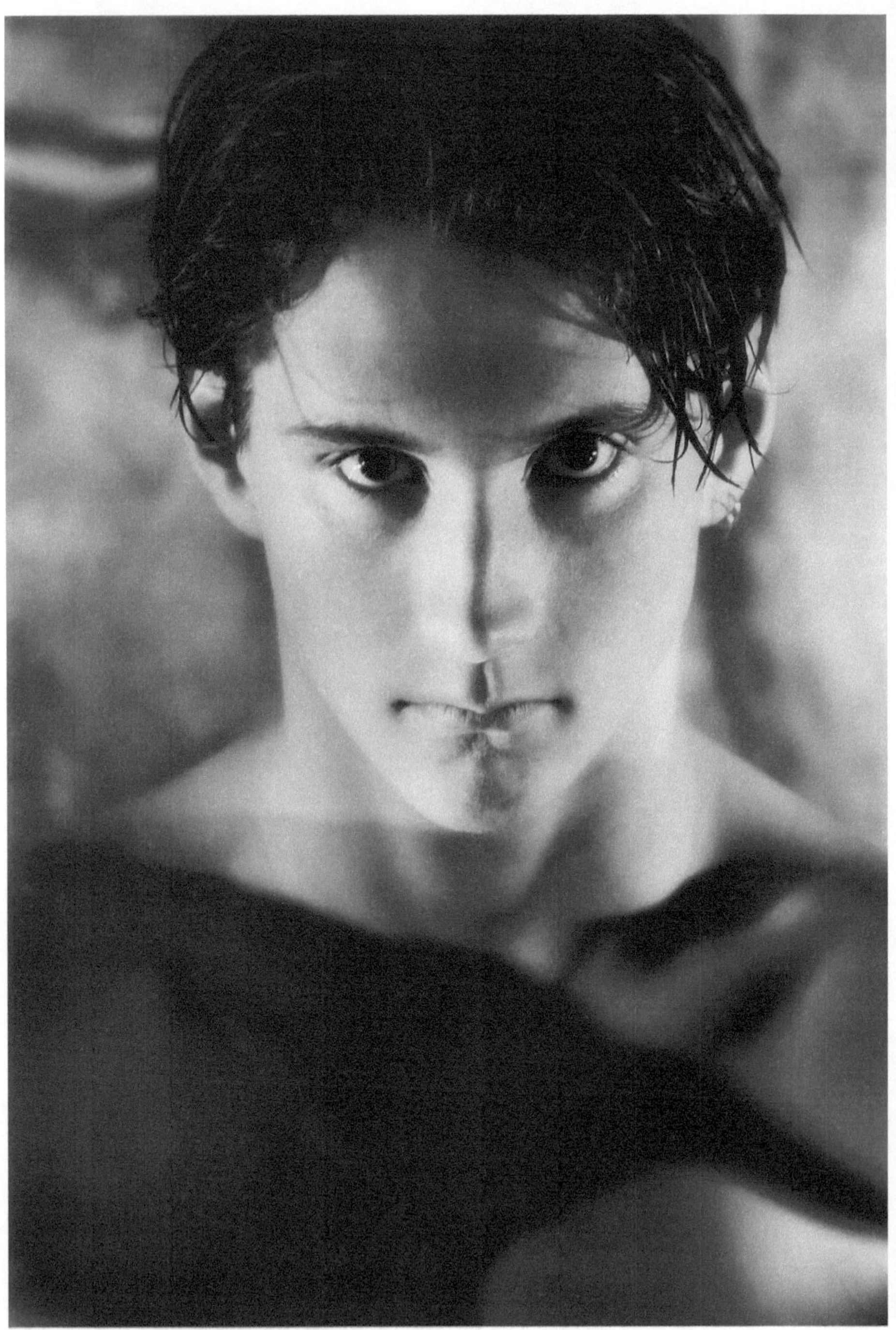

Portrait of a Youth, photograph, 1992

Will he

lean the question of death
on the trigger in my throat
as he begs me to take him
higher
and higher?

Will I?

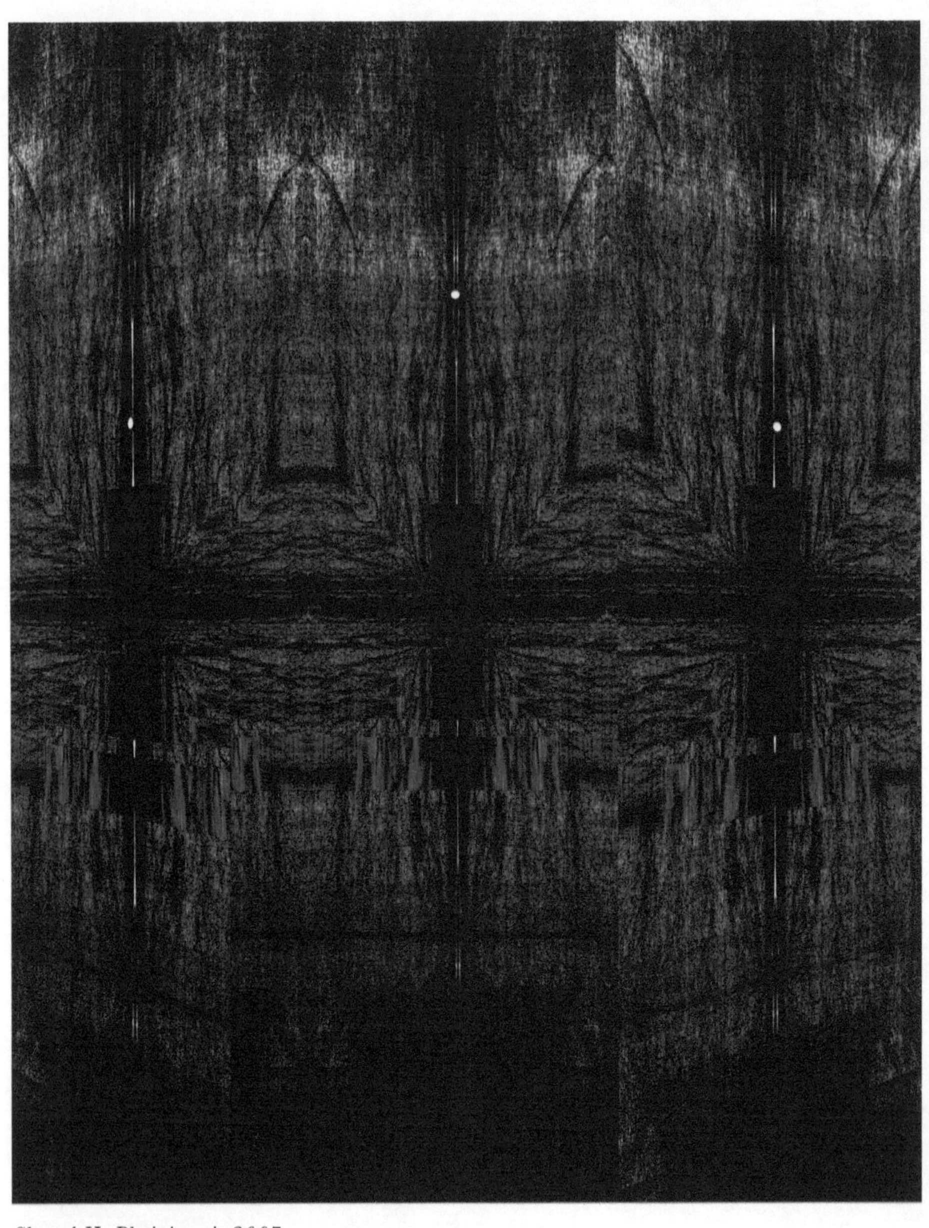

Shroud II, Phainiomai, 2007

Adagio

On the seventh day of the seventh moon
the heart's ocean bled into life and ascended.

More than once, I fed this bird of flight,
this lover of light, to capture

that fluid of song
in this blue jar, I keep

under the stairs
beneath the stars.

The Portrait

All day I think of his face
coming into the light,
his eyes fixed on the emptiness of the room.
I breathe
and he smiles.

Does he sense the uncertain spaces I've set aside?
The possibilities?

I'm thinking:
the eventuality of passion,
a playfield of irresistible madness.
His beauty shakes loose, and for this moment, I would die
for penetration, flesh into flesh,
fantastic fruit, pooling of sweat,
salty-sweet and strange.

It's true.
I'm balancing the dark and light of invention,
tending to the fables of the heart.

Will he move me
with the soaring heat of his thighs
or leave me only dreaming of passion,
astounded by the image, the fabulous
drinking of his eyes?

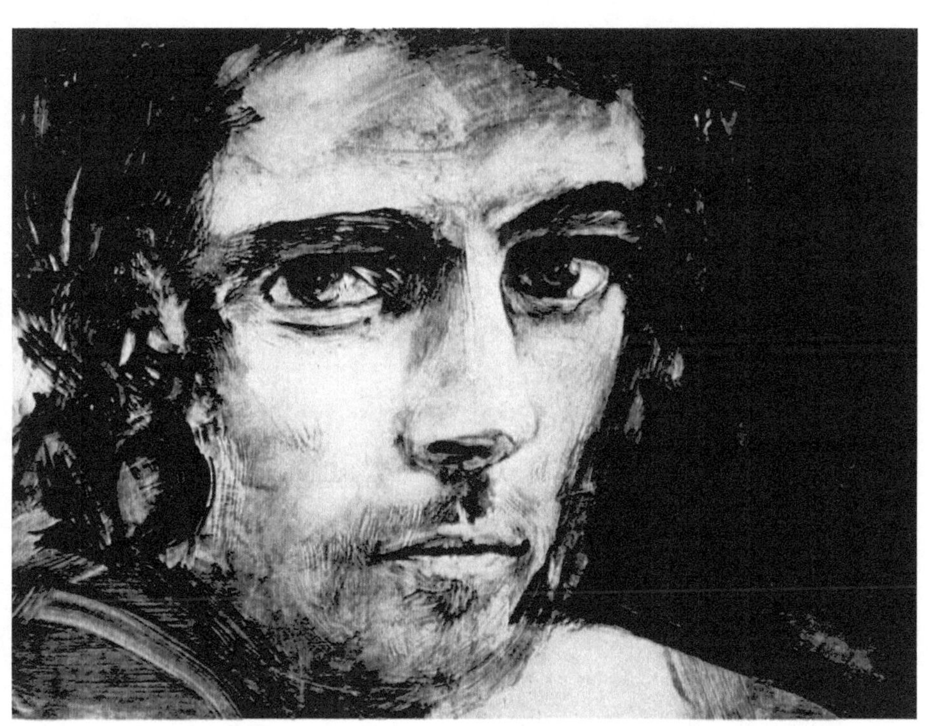

Portrait of a Young Poet, monotype, ca 1994

The Fall of Clues

I

Things that might happen:
It could rain, or the door you open goes nowhere.

Things happen: before you know it, the pain of loss
when nothing is lost. It never
happens, yet it does.
You hook everything to memory—the smell of wind woven
from the loom of childhood, the heaving
beaches and blue water, distant
voices that curve across yellow dunes.

You remember your child self soaring
above the sand and how you measured the shadow
your body made in the sun.
You remember the pale sky's invisible moon.

And one day, when everything meets
in the perfect tense, something imagined will happen.
It happens. You drift into the sea,
into the perfect turbulence
of God's imperfect eye.

Darkness. This day of your death.
Sand and shadows
of late afternoon light.

You've stumbled into your past
falling upon descending clues,
imagining a life you'd live again,
just as you dreamed you might.

II

I remember each word you said. I remember
the warm air that lingered inside
the room and the bed that held us.

Your intoxicating soft-curved inner thighs turning,
and I, floating and tremulous, drinking up the dark heat,
made the journey over and over again
drunk on the taut, drum-like beauty of your skin.

Your low-throated laughter swam through the darkness
above my heart, my head above your loins, that
part of me growing to a pinnacle of desire,
until the press and thrum of wings slid away.

Filled of your sea and released of fire, I surrendered
to the heaving dunes of your body, here
on the raft of sleep, beneath the invisible moon.

For Hephaiston

You are
my second self,
brother of my heart and keeper
of my breath.

You are
my other self, my lover in battle
and we breathe in
all of this world together.

You are
a vessel of space, virtuous
shape of my heart, grace
of starlight

You are
my champion and everything
turns with the turning of your face and your smile.
Do not leave this life
without me.

To A Lover

You move your body across the room
with the slow rhythm of a rolling ship
upon the sea, like no ship I've seen,
nor will ever see.

Your golden prow gathers the light
of my one desire.

Wave upon wave
    collapses.

Stars are made of fire, but none burn brighter
than the folding in of you, pulsing heat
against my body

Paidika

I am the proper erastes with my beautiful Eromenos
here at my side. He amuses himself
with my gifts of silver and scarlet combs.
I encourage him to speak highly of himself.
Let us all applaud his good looks,
his youthful body in bloom, his smooth breast
and brave thighs, his carefree heart.
And where he now lies, beneath the trees,
I shall make sacred this space, a place to come
and speak to friends of his innocence and his bravery.
For them all, I will share, like this bread,
a dear recollection: The sweet smell of pine
upon his hair.

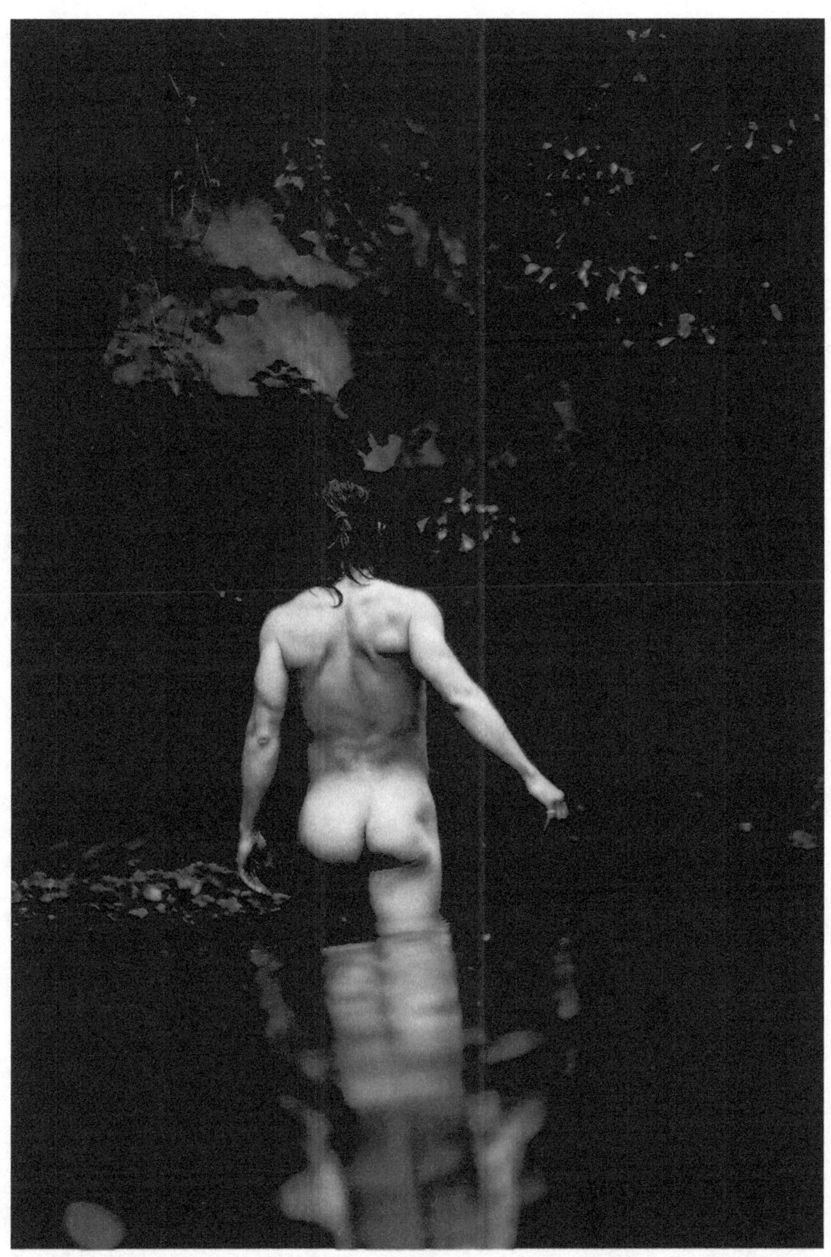

Figure in the Lake, photograph, Sicily, ca 1996

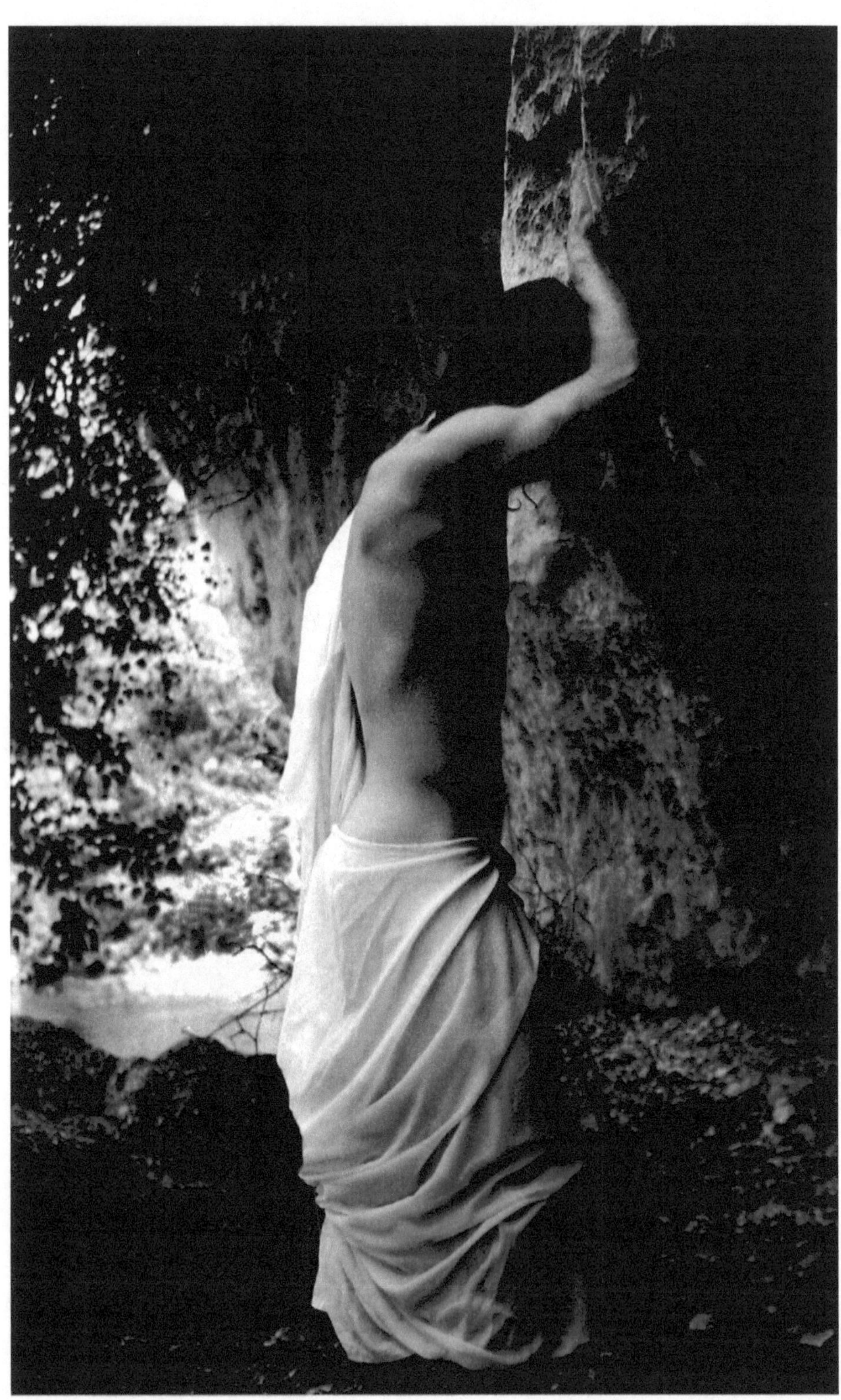

Christopher in Sicily, 1996

Spindle of the Eye

for James Broughton

In the eventuality of remembrance
the balancing eye marries the heart
at the mouth of words.
The image and the silence of the image
broken by the idea.
The cradle of the arm
into which his head sinks
is the perfect parenthetical gesture.
Can you see it?
Can you feel the eye balance the heart
until the silence of the image is finally broken by word?
The cradling of the arm into which his head sinks.
And where does the verticality of the cliff,
re-described in the soft, shadowed flesh of the body, fall?
The axis of arm and head,
lines of light striking stone and thigh, the tumbling
river's bright water, the trembling leaves, and the gossamer folds
of fabric flowing across the smooth skin of his body,
the ambiguities of place, of black
and white, and the pewter distillation of sky.
Words converge in the beauty of idea and the idea of beauty—
a confluence of descending possibilities.
Is this it?
Where everything reached is caught
in the rapture of the question?

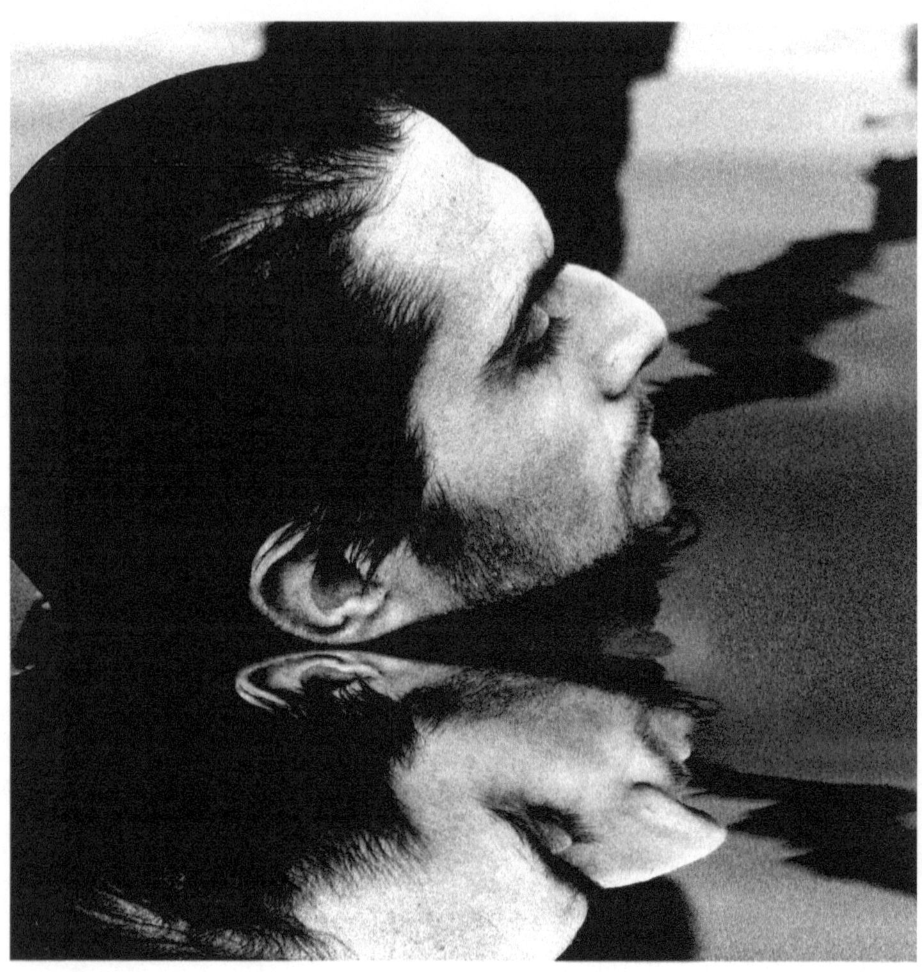

What I Remember, photograph, 2014

The Fisher King

I'm fishing for a fundamental metaphor,
supple transference of a noble idea
regarding your body, the way it swims
in and out, across
that spectacular sea of possibility.
I suffer no poverty of hope but feast
upon this absolute belief: the heart is an ocean
into which we fall
headlong, thrashing through a panoply of cliches
and, like a blind man, tripping on dog-eared similes.
Yet, it is here, the heart,
pulse of imperfection, and the tides of hope,
where the confluence of desire
and what is left of it
slowly sink away.
The world spins too quickly, waters
evaporate, and hunger of the flesh diminish.
The metaphor cannot be caught,
only glimpsed as it breaches
its rhyme and rhythm. I would
abandon all conventions if I could;
I would invent an unsaid, unseen something
from the deepest part of me,
about you and for you,
something impossibly rare
and rising.

The Actor

For Richard Svare

From the shade of the temple, the actor
pushes out and crosses the streets. Even
here in the Plaka, he must forever tighten his lines;
he must always consider the intervals of ideas.
There is yet another play to learn.
It is noon, and the cruel sun accuses him of forgetfulness.
He can't imagine where he's been in this life
to suffer such heat and debris. And for whom, he wonders,
and why here have my gods set me down to dry up.

He shops for books, butter and bread, good
wine, then heads homeward over the hot dusty stones
through the crowd. He is grateful
to slip into the coolness of his private rooms, thankful
for the darkness. He is alone, and silence swallows him.
Everywhere there is something placed with care.
An empty clay bowl sits
near the center of a small table.
Full of my life it sits, he muses, with what

is left of his metaphysical humor.
In Athens, the August heat has been ruthless.
The actor opens a new script.
It is an old play, one of love and lovers.
He is meant to be Skythinos, the poet, erastes
to Elissos, whose youthful beauty eclipsed all
others and whose heart was full of courage.
In the end, of course, Elisos falls prey to the sharp
and bitter blade of another fair youth
in the heat of jealousy.

Skythinos holds the dead Elissos. It is a last tender kiss
of words. "We once held each other in the loins of Eros.
You were ripe and ready for love, and I wrote a poem
each day on the gift of your grace. Your voice
held my name with tender perfection.
Elissos, how have we met so in parting?
Gone now. And I am left among the burning embers
of all these gods."

You

You might not be pleased
to be placed at the top
without a name.
(I thought I could name you.)

Higher still,
I'd place you beyond the moon and sun,
perhaps a distant planet
that has no name for night.

Suspended in the heavens on this page,
you, with all this white around you,
would rather not be hung above the debris
of my expectation, the kick and cantered
slant of thoughts. The rumination,
and ranting,

The mad clutter marching from border to border,
anxious leap of
        indentation,
the clattering of stops and starts,
of exclamatory avowals,
parenthetical swells that rise
toward something untouchable and beautiful.

You wish to be
cut loose.
I know.

And I wonder what is needed to dismantle
the perfect muse. Will you
evaporate? How
and where will you go?

Which part dies first? The heart?
The face?
The music?
The weight of hope would be nice,
but, like arsenic in the blood,
it lingers.

I don't blame you.

What is beautiful must flee from those
who make it beautiful.
Always.
Had I named you,
I might not have known you,
just so.

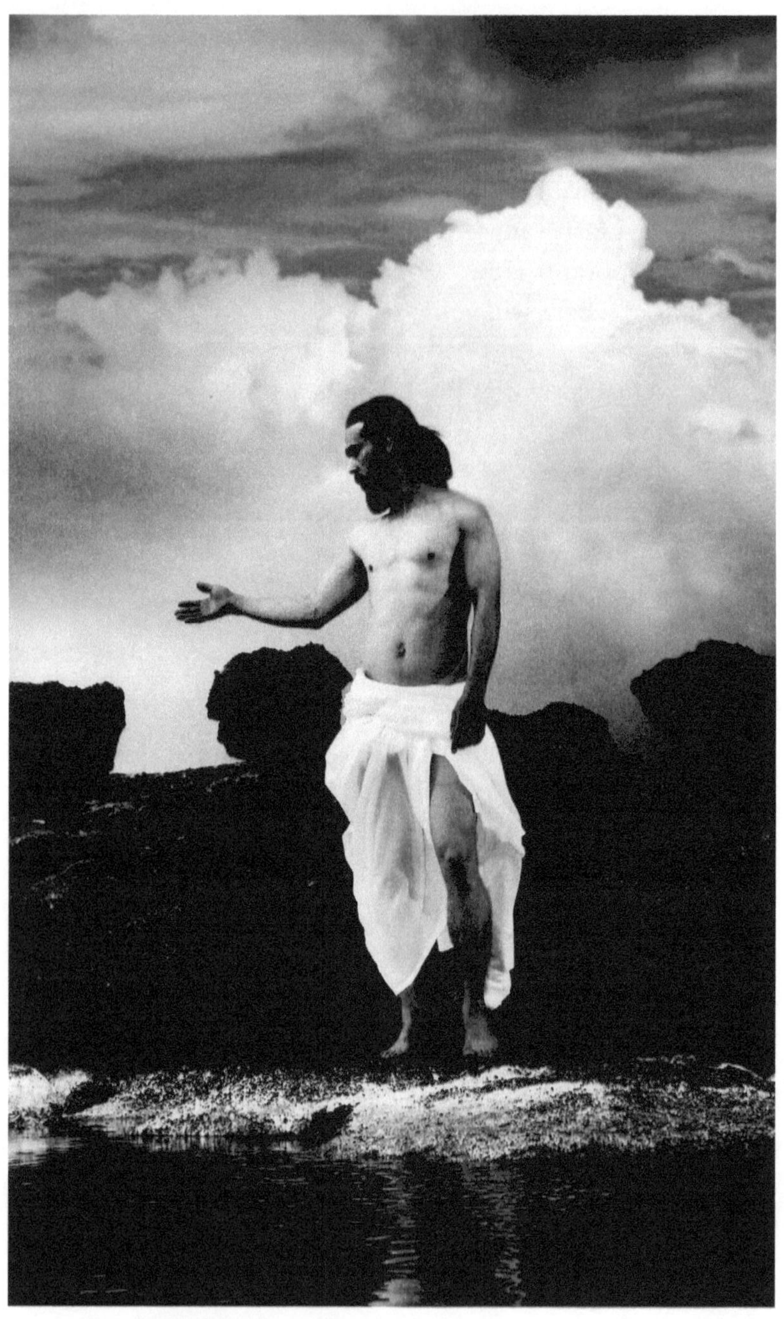

The Prophet, photograph, Crete 1996

Eo Nomine Eo Nomine

Jesus came out of my house at night, walking
across the barren yard. He gathered the light of my torch
and studied the stones
        that held the gate.
"These stones," he said, "have come from across the river, far
from here. They are of a color
unlike those which have made my house
        safe from the sins of my Father."

Jesus said, "When I was a woman in the desert, I wanted
to follow a path
to my Father's hearth,
to fuel the earth and make
      his bed a bridal bed,
but he sent me back into the desert with my blood
      and fed me stones.
He made me a man for his heaven."

Jesus knelt before the base of the gate. "Look!
In the veins of the rock. What you see
is old and smooth as dreams. In the dreams
you take desire into the light, and from this light
shape all meaning."

Jesus rose and turned.
He put his hands out
      against the sky,
as if to hold back the inevitable curtain, the falling
debris of his death. He left
for Qumran with only John Mark,
      his heavenly wife.

Glory

The glory of Jesus blooms in eternal grace;
the glory of his illuminated face radiates
into the hearts of humankind.

To set eyes upon such countenance,
is to swim in the deepness of his kiss.

Jesus, pushing away the dark night, sings,
"Spirit and body are one. Taste of me
now. Your heaven is here."

The glory of Jesus is the body-passionate,
magnetic, swollen with the blood of humankind.

The villagers come to the font of his loins
and slake their thirst in the glory of his seed,
impregnated of this world and not another.
"Look into my eyes and see yourself each a Kingdom,
a paradigm of hope. I will comfort you
as you bathe in this reflection. Let no one stand
empty of this eternal fire."

In Qumran, Holy city of the Essenes,
old and young wait beneath the cooling palms. Jesus
leads them to the cistern, all circling
without speaking, the noon sun bearing down
without restraint,
witness to the daily absolution.
Each one bathes a part of Jesus
kissing it, then naming it.

Jesus, in turn, bathes each supplicant.
"Let me take you now and fill you with wonderment.
Let me plow your soul
with this eternal moment, this timeless spirit.
Your body is an empty vessel
in the sea of desire.
Let me fill it."

A Love Poem

Between living one's life and dying one's death, between
one life and another, between the dark and light patterns
that feed and steady our vision of what comes and goes,
of what has been before us and of what we believe will follow,
between the first real hunger and the last meal of the man
who is made criminal for the color of his love,
there is a line drawn upon line and then upon another, erased
and redrawn, hung from the swirling red light
of the womb to the black and white bloodless tomb. The sky
is blue and forgiving of my doubts.
I have drawn upon your face
the faintest flower of hope
for your beauty and your love.

Narcissus

I know what I look like.
I think I know what I look like,
if I look like
what I want to look like.

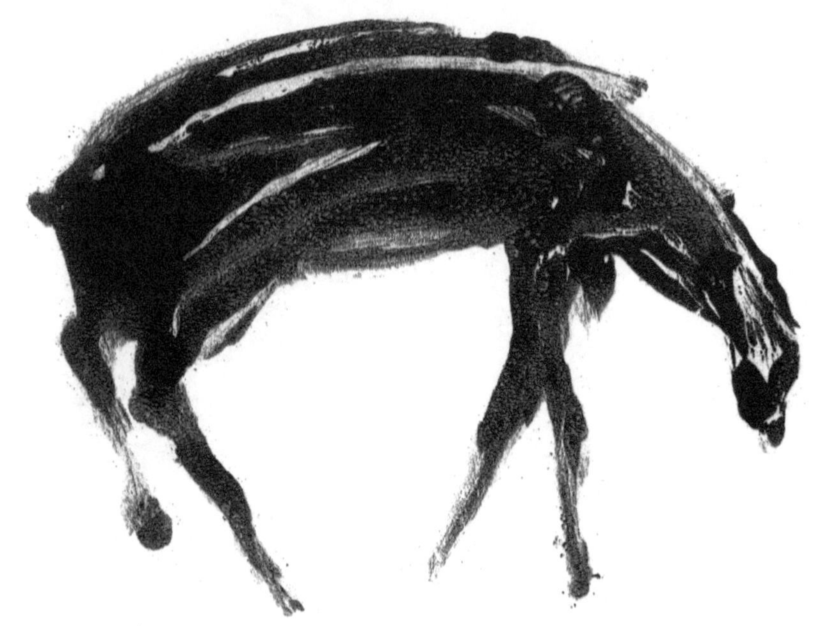

Deer, monotype, 1982

Champion

What champion legs, rising
up and running from long shadows
his body leaves. Shadows that tear
at nothing but the empty, blue air he stirs.

In the swiftness of his flight, he breathes in
late yellow sky boned of clouds, his beating
heart beats a measured pace, then the slowing
deer-like turn of foot and grace before this arrow
and his world meet.

I could have saved this shaft for another
and let his dreams unfold. I could have
spared his heart, this champion of beauty
who beats a century of glory in every pump
of that heavenly cock, in every toss
and turn of thigh.

But hunger falls between us; the gloss of love
is washed in blood. Could I, whose loins
ache for such immeasurable honor,
have made my world without him?

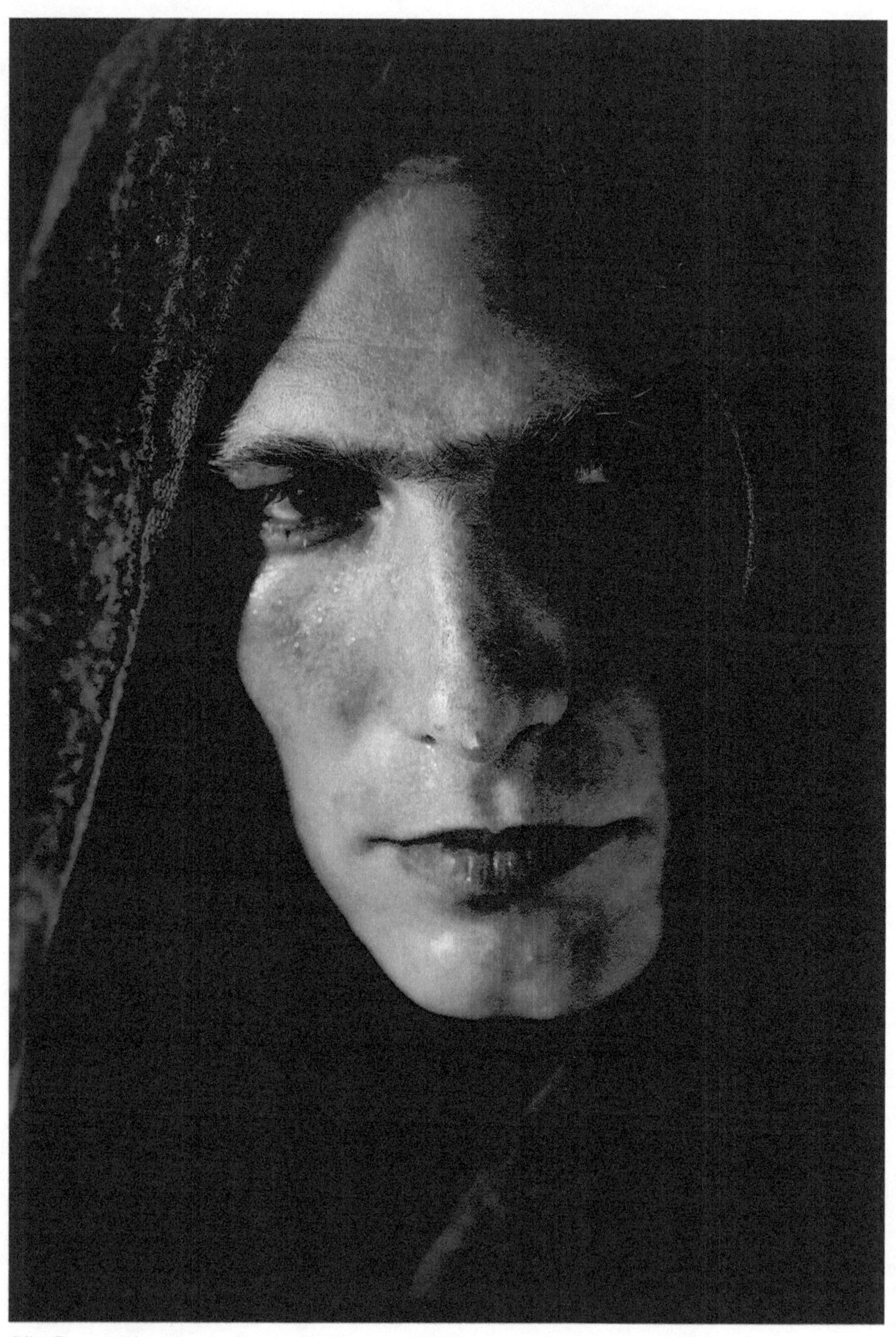

The Boxer, photograph, Savannah, Georgia 1987

Encounter

This moment drifts
by the heights of his cheekbones
where my thoughts sit
like rocks on a cliff, until he lifts me
higher still with one cautious
yet irrepressible smile.

Isham

No one saw me die.
No one saw me in the rain and
no one came to sing.
No dances given, no lamps lit.

I passed through the storm
a dying flame. No one
called my name.

Still, you found me breathing
in the waters of hope.

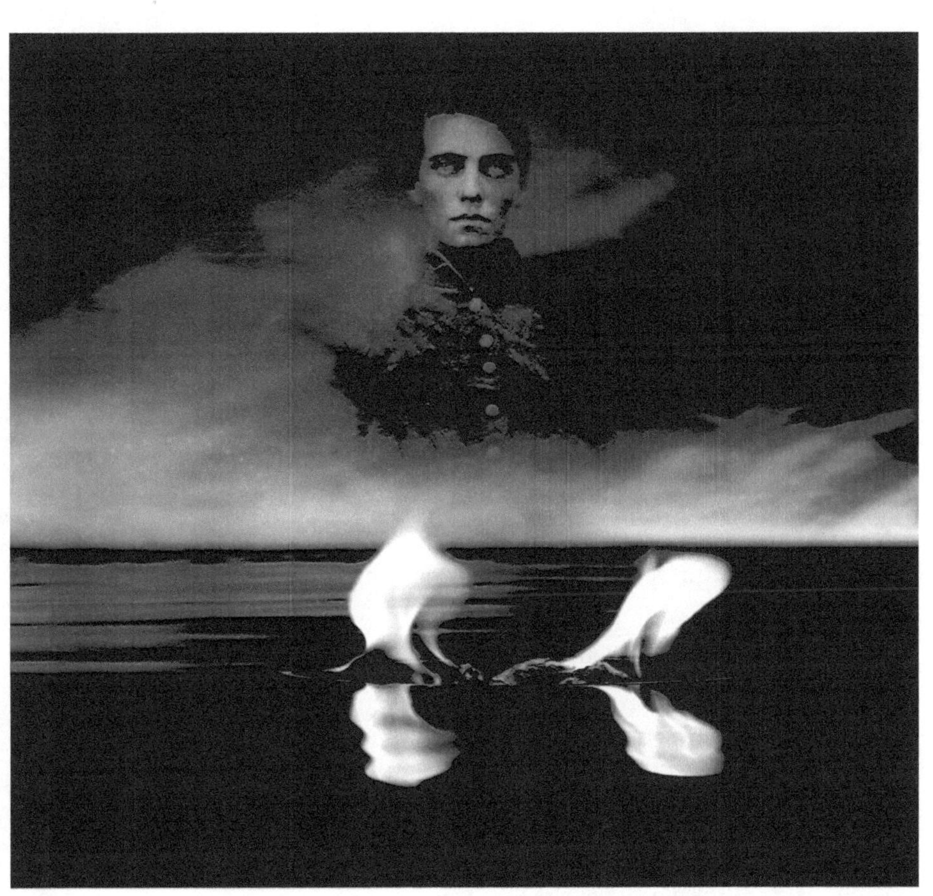

The Burial of Isham Lane, from Dream Sea, 2016

Temple

Yours is a temple rushing upward
colliding light,
dark columnar heat of thighs.

Night hangs here
in this soft-petaled present.
You move me with a word, a world

of hunger consumes me, dreams
of passion, burnished green
and gold, turning us

in heaven's heat upon the altar.
It is the same old dream, the same
remarkable face, generative body, made holy,

palpable, irresistible,
your shape a shadow perfected
in the chase.

It is always the same.
The mercy of night is my beginning, your flesh
my flower, blooming of fire and ice.

Another Place

Would you let me take you
to another world, between
here and there, far beyond
what you've ever imagined,
a place of water and dreams,
of long light where it seems
we've lived forever...if I could?

RUMINATIONS

WAITING FOR SAMSARA

This morning, a mass of black clouds spilled over Mt. Suthep, enshrouding the temple's golden chedi overlooking the city of Chiang Mai. Warm, torrential rain followed. It's July, and I'm hunkered down in my unbelievably small studio, mulling over an unwanted blue passage, listening to Jami Sieber's 'Hidden Sky,' alternately gazing through the open door, then contemplating the subtle desiccation of skin that has sheathed me for six decades. It's incredible. Not necessarily chiming in at sixty, but the multi-processing of the human mind—a mass of black, rain, blue, open, space, withering, skin, connecting, what works, what doesn't, placing and holding—all of these a continuum of ideas, words—this letter.

Nearing sixty is no particular miracle. Or is it? More people haven't made it than have if you consider the average life span of the human through history and that young men have always been fodder for war; there has never been a time when, somewhere, a battle wasn't devouring our youth. Or has there?

Where I live, one might consider it a miracle just to survive the traffic. Almost daily, I pass the white-chalked outline of a motorbike or of a body or the drying pool of blood of a careless youth too lazy or too drunk to bother to put on a protective helmet. Most fatalities occur at night, not precisely because of alcohol but because the police only enforce the helmet law during daytime working hours. For the young, it's a question of fashion and hairstyle. Hair spiked with styling gel suffers pitifully under a sweaty helmet.

I have thus far escaped cancer, tuberculosis, malaria, starvation, floods, and countless other leveling agents of the human species. I've yet to be eliminated by an act of terrorism, though the chances grow daily. As an American living in a foreign country, I'm acutely aware that my country is being held hostage by the current political administration, hawkish thugs more interested in money than what America should be. Whether they dress in Christian ideology or patriotism, they are modern-day oligarchs of the worst sort. For them, putting out a fire means throwing more petrol on it. After all, they have a keen interest in fuel.

What happens to the mind and the body at sixty that didn't happen at fifty or forty? One is closer to seventy and the great beyond of gravity into which we've deposited such a rich accumulation of myth.

We experience the concept of 'now,' 'this moment,' and 'the present as potentiality. The past swiftly eradicates everything. When we speak of this moment, we speak of the nearest mentally registered event in the continuum of our memory, which we call our past. This idea is essential when turning sixty because everything past is non-existent. We all know the future doesn't exist because it hasn't yet happened. If I blink at the precise nanosecond, I won't be any older. I like that. The Buddha teaches us to live in the present moment, does he not?

Even so, we tend to thrust ourselves forward on past ruminations. On turning sixty, I have not so seriously calculated how much I devoted my life to being an artist. All of it? In some ways, yes. But when I consider the places where I have made and sold art, I'd estimate about forty years. Considering the arc of developing intensity in one's career, eating, sleeping, sex, and other miscellaneous social habits and biological functions, I've actively processed and actualized creative ideas for approximately 5000 days. Modest enough. I'm not an obsessive artist. Twenty thousand hours or 7,200,000 minutes or 43,200,000 seconds or 43,200,000,000,000,000 (quadrillion) nanoseconds of fishing around in the unknown and then serving up the results to the world. Why? Why, indeed, my unkind critics might pen. But my 'why' is the greater 'why.' Some folks believe that creativity comes from a need to stoke the ego's furnace, but art can become a moral compass once delivered to us. Others claim a personal dance with the collective consciousness spirals the artist into that sublime act. I don't know. Why I make art is not the same reason we need art. Yet, the two are inseparable.

The difficulty of being a modern-day painter is that we are utterly alone in our subjective world, struggling to connect our fabricated reality to something more significant, and we have no stick with which to measure our purpose and the result, except what we choose to believe and what others choose to tell us.

The good or the lousy painting has less to do with the craft of the work, which might fail in its craftsmanship, but will succeed in its honesty. I've seen artwork that would miss the mark in almost everything we were taught in art academia but resonate in honesty, seriousness, and vulnerability. Primitivism and Outsider Art offer us the best examples. Some painters are technical wizards in image-making, but the art is dead. There are still many who have neither craft nor honesty.

Every act of painting is an engagement with uncertainty. Images slowly appear from the studio, which was once a maid's room tucked away in the upper corner of the house. The new work imbues the spirit of Buddha, which gives me comfort, despite the constant intrusion of the ego and the equally constant battle to keep it at a safe distance. Of course, one can only partially accomplish this, but doing so takes me to the unexpected.

I've never felt a need to be prolific, and I've never felt that being so has anything to do with art. I have no idea how many paintings I've created; I've made a few good ones. After forty years or so, one should believe in oneself. Someone once told me that artists are the least able to judge the merits of our creative output; this is true to some extent in that the proximity of the work itself easily shapes our judgments. But always, at some point, the artist should know, better than anyone, whether they succeeded or failed.

At any rate, even at sixty, the more important thing to consider is what I still need to create. My thoughts are akin to those of my painter friend Lennie Kesl. Nearing eighty, he talks about the work he wants to get done before he dies. He's already left a prodigious and eclectic assortment of genuinely exciting art. Yet he still searches for that one inexpressible painting.

The rains have come and gone. The shadows in the room grow sharper and darker. The sky holds a pearl of white, like the color of a morning lotus. The blue passage is now mostly scrubbed away to memory, mostly buried beneath an avalanche of black, which, in turn, will be washed away. I'm grateful to be here at sixty. I'm in better health than I've been in years. Of course, the skin has begun its journey southward, but it has been a good friend, and I have no complaints.

Everything is reductive and rearranged by prayer, myth, and, finally, by this illusion of time—everything except our extraordinary potential for life expressing itself in each eternal now moment. It is enough, I think, to sit by the river and become water.

The Fisherman

He sat on the rocks by the river
his robes hiked high, legs
paddling the water,
his tired feet dancing in the current
among the fish and gray-blue stones.

"Make no mistake," he said, "I'm no messiah,
not at all, and no cause
for celebration. I am not a god.
Don't be stupid. I'm the same as you—
amply mortal, a pod full of shit, seeds,
and stardust, yet more sacred than any myth."

All at once he rolled back upon a boulder,
his bare azimuthal knees fluttering
like a butterfly in the wind. Trapped
in his remarkably prehensile feet,
twisted a magnificent carp.

"Let's eat," said the Master,
"Let's eat."

Do Elephants Paint?

Elephants began their evolutionary history at about the same time as humans. Both species probably began as herbivores, but somewhere far back in that implacable flight in which we separated ourselves from other species, we stood and turned significantly toward a more varied bill of fare; we added meat to our diet. While the elephants kept grazing and getting bigger, the two-legged human got leaner and meaner. Undoubtedly, we owe our current status as 'resident bullies' to the enormous caloric barbeques these creatures provided. Between climatic changes and our voracious appetite, the elephant's ancestors, the mastodon and wooly mammoth disappeared millennia ago, about the same time humans began their profession as painters, the first stirrings of cross-referencing reality. Since early humans kept no record, no one knows with certainty. Still, it's believed cave paintings, such as those in Roufflignac, Altamira, or Lascaux, were highly ritualized pre-enactments of a later, actual event to ensure a successful kill; meat on the table, a brand-new coat and a bit of jewelry. And proboscides were at the top of the menu.

In these vast, dark caves of Paleolithic Europe, early man created stunning images of creatures it liked to eat; here, too, no doubt came the spawning of religion and insurance companies. These primitive images coalesced with objects of fertility; sex, then life, then death, which gave us Egyptian artifacts and Greek sculpture, Roman temples, Gothic churches, Michelangelo's Capello Sistina, the horrific visions of Goya, Monet's haystacks, Picasso's bulls, Abstract Expressionism, and the Campbell Soup Cans by Andy Warhol.

What were elephants doing all this time to satisfy their artistic spirit? They bypassed all this convoluted, symbolic 'stuff' and ate. They need to; They're big and inefficient processors of food. Much of what goes in comes back out without much benefit to the elephant but is a healthy advantage to numerous other species.

Besides, what creature has time to think about making art when it must keep packing in kilos of fodder and liters of water? A wild bull elephant eats enough vegetation daily to equal the weight of about two humans. Imagine if they were carnivores.

Or perhaps they never had the angst we have that propels our exigency to create. Though they have every reason, humans have just about eliminated them. In the latter part of the twentieth century, statistically, one elephant was murdered every hour over a decade. In the last few years, media hype has exploded about elephants' newly discovered artistic abilities. They paint with the energy and style of a William De Kooning or Franz Kline and play various musical instruments. Dave Soldier, co-creator of the world's only elephant orchestra, seems convinced that elephants can extemporize music; he considers this as 'writing' music. He believes elephants enjoy human music and like to play it. Doing so helps raise money for their upkeep, and Soldier sees no problem with the elephant's transition from logging to show business.

As an artist, I've been curious about all of this. Also, for the last four years, I've been working on an independent film project in Thailand to understand the extraordinary relationship between humans and captive elephants and raise funds for conservancy and educative awareness.

I have mixed feelings about elephants painting and playing musical instruments. On the one hand, elephants playing in an orchestra or painting lyrical abstractions is pure and simple entertainment for humans. Elephants are just one of many animals we've used and abused long before the Romans perfected the concept of zoos and circuses. One subspecies of the African elephant was brought to extinction during the ancient Roman Empire's relentless passion for ivory, constructing vast palaces from the teeth of these creatures.

On the other hand, where the conundrum begins to blister, these are projects set up by humans meant to help the captive elephants. The problems of captive elephants are different from those of wild elephants. Most importantly, you cannot let a captive elephant loose into the wild, even if there were enough 'wild' out there. They've been bonded to humans, and we cannot undo that complicated psychological relationship without creating additional problems for elephants and ourselves.

To better understand the painting project and to filter out my feelings, I took the opportunity and invitation to work with the 'painting' elephants at the Elephant Conservation Center in Lampang, Thailand. This foundation is the group with which Kolmar and Malamud dazzled the public in their highly sensationalized book "When Elephants Paint." I wasn't interested in when they paint or how they paint but do they paint. In other words, do they conscientiously make art the way we do?

The process is necessarily and extensively collaborative. My job was to mix the colors and load the brush with pigment for the mahout, who placed the paintbrush in the elephant's trunk. The elephant applies the paint, the mahout selects another color, and so on. An essential part of my job is to indicate when the painting is complete. The mahout often, though not always, influences the actual painting process, pushing the trunk left or right, guiding a tusk, or occasionally using vocal commands.

And yet, the elephant often applies pigment with conscientious determination, and elephant painters, like human painters, have their particular style. Pong's interest in creating enclosed, parenthetical shapes has been consistent throughout his painting career. His stroke application differed significantly from Wanatee's Cezannesque vertical slashes, which looked uncannily like the forest before her. Some prefer painting more than others, and some seem more gifted. And some, like the charming Prathida, who was once a star painter, find the whole brush and paint thing rather dull these days. He does it, but one gets the feeling that for him, it's just another dumb job assigned by the humans. If elephants like to paint because they get bored in captivity, as some argue, they would quickly get bored from repetition. These creatures paint for tourists twice a day, seven days a week, a job, I'm sure, they didn't sign up for willingly.

The project I was involved in had nothing to do with the tourist shows but rather to produce paintings sold over National Geographic's Novica site. The project has been financially very successful in bringing much-needed income into the Conservation Center. The cost of keeping one elephant is expensive. The Center has over fifty elephants; each has been assigned at least one mahout, and the mahout has a family he must feed and clothe. And, of course, the administrative cost lies above it all.

If I didn't call an end to the painting, would the elephant continue making the painting as long as it's given a loaded brush? If so, does this mean the elephant is never given a chance to express itself fully? And would a 'professional' elephant pick up a brush and paint away even if no human was present? These might seem like ridiculous questions, but are they? Everything is predicated on our sense of esthetics and desires, not the elephants.' We want the painting to please us, not other elephants. We have yet to learn what the elephant is thinking or what it wants. We have enough difficulty communicating between ourselves, our culture, and our race, let alone other species. And we might not want to know what the elephants express through their painting. Ok, you say, "Lighten up! This project is all for the ultimate benefit of the elephants because they are rapidly disappearing from the planet, and there are no real jobs for captive elephants since we've over-logged the forest while at the same time destroying the natural habitat for the few remaining wild elephants. Without tourism supporting the relationship between the captive elephant and the human, they will surely disappear. Projects like elephant paintings and elephant orchestras keep the public focused on the serious dilemma of the elephant." But do they? Is it enough to merely purchase a CD of an elephant orchestra or a painting by an elephant? Can and should we do more? Richard lair, Director of the Special Projects for the Elephant Conservation Center, believes that elephants should never have been made captive in the first place. After being a beast of burden for over five thousand years, they remain essentially wild and have never been genetically altered for domesticity, making their relationship with us rather remarkable; we have bound them to us out of fear, love, and trust. He believes that, sadly, without tourism, there is no hope for the captive elephant. If this is so, it is only a temporary palliative for an alarming problem, not just in Thailand but worldwide and not just with elephants.

I frantically raced between Pong and Prathida, loading their brushes with the colors I liked because elephants are colorblind. Since I had two elephants painting, two mahouts assisting, ten brushes bristling, and twenty pots of paint drying, it took a lot of work to be judicious in determining if a painting was complete. For me, it hardly mattered. What mattered was being amid their great breathing and quiet spirit, so utterly palpable in this world. It's difficult not to be filled with absolute joy and astonishment when you're so close to these magnificent beings and difficult not to wonder what is to become of them. And, as well, I wonder what is to become of us.

How and why have elephants embedded themselves so deeply in the human psyche? Is it because we share many biological and sociological traits or have a similar lifespan? Or that we are prone to suffer many of the same physical ailments, that we have similar familial constructs, or that, as a species, we both alter the environment in which we live. Perhaps the elephant knows more about this than we do.

Now that I've painted with the elephants, have my feelings changed or at least become more focused? Perhaps I should not have titled this essay with the question, "Do elephants paint?" Any answer can be too easily wrestled away in semantics. A more critical question: should they paint? But this, too, is problematic.

We need to be more united in our thinking about captive elephants. PETA (People for the Ethical Treatment of Animals), a beneficial advocacy organization, often prone to tossing the baby out with the bathwater, would no doubt consider even the idea of an elephant painting as abusive. On the other side are groups like the Feld Corporation, who own circuses and avidly promote elephant breeding programs under benign species conservancy, but, in reality, breeding more elephants to entertain more people and make more money. Floating in the middle are the adherents to the archaic institution of the zoo. Zoos spend a lot of money trying not to be considered circuses while convincing us how much we need them. We don't. We need sanctuaries for animals that we've caged for too long. No one needs to see an animal locked in a sterile cage to learn how that animal would live if it were free.

If elephant paintings can temporarily help stabilize captive elephants' precarious condition, then ok. But it's a sad fix, and we must be careful. It is too easy to exploit the elephant, even under the guise of helping it. Humans have established dominion over these gentle giants for over fifty thousand years. We eat them, and we enslave them. We make them entertain us. We demolish their spirit and wear their teeth. During the Vietnamese War, pilots were instructed to blow up elephants lest they might carry some assistance to the enemy. Even today, elephants inadvertently step on land mines. We poison, strangle, drown, and electrocute them for encroaching on land once their land. And yet, paradoxically, we worship them; we love them. What a curious creature is the human. The essayist Loren Eisley suggested that all species are born with an ordainment of extinction. Maybe the dinosaur did become extinct from the cataclysmic collision of an asteroid with planet Earth, and quite possibly, elephants will vanish from the insatiable appetite of over-populating Homo sapiens.
And what will become of us, creatures who stood in caves so long ago, making art with one hand and war with the other? While we readily fly the banner of supreme intelligence, we could easily suffer an inglorious disappearance from our greed and stupidity. I hope not, and I hope, for our sake, the elephants remain with us; they shouldn't have to paint to do so.

February 24th, 2003

Wind At The Edge of the Heart
Thoughts on Van Gogh and Ourselves

During the spring of 1967, on my way to lunch in the Student Union Building at the University of Alaska in Fairbanks, I saw then read a recently published Popular Science magazine on a table in the lobby that featured a story about a new French invention. The article described a device that used infrasonic sound waves controlled in such a way as to emit varying degrees of intensity, and, depending on the level, the weapon could cause vomiting, fainting, seizures, and even death. The scientists had discovered these ultra-low frequencies in the prevalent winds of southern France, known as the Mistrals.

I was particularly excited about stumbling across this article. As a student of painting and music, I had no interest in weapons and, at the time, little interest in science, but I was captivated by what I read. Like many young art students, I was fascinated by the French Expressionist Vincent Van Gogh. Perhaps it was the overall tragedy of his life ending so young. What other artist looms so large an archetype of a suffering, creative genius? I read everything I could get my hands on, including his letters, most of which were to his brother Theo. There were numerous letters about Vincent, most notably from the French painter Paul Gauguin who briefly lived with Vincent in Arles, France.

I felt I had stumbled upon my little Rosetta Stone. No one has ever been able to give a precise reason for Van Gogh's journey into madness and ultimate suicide. It has often been suggested that he had epilepsy. When treated in 1889, two doctors diagnosed Vincent with epilepsy—seizures consisting of acute mania with sensory hallucinations, particularly affecting sight and hearing. However, there is no indication of epilepsy before he arrives in Arles. Still, others have long argued that his daily intake of absinthe drove him over the edge. Absinthe is a strong alcoholic drink made partly with a poisonous, hallucinogenic ingredient called wormwood. I tend to agree that the latter is the stronger candidate, but, in my opinion, it was a combination of everything—the absinthe, his upbringing, genetic imprints, and his environment, i.e., the winds.

In a letter to Theo, Vincent recounted that when he first arrived in Arles, as he was getting off the train, a man getting on the train advised him to return to wherever he came from because, quite simply, the people in Arles were a bit strange. Not unusual; similar behavior has long been reported in other areas where extreme winds prevail over long periods, causing anxiety and depression among residents.

It should be noted that Van Gogh did not cut off his entire ear. He merely sliced off a portion. Some say the helix, the upper part of the external ear, and some say the lobule, the ear lobe. In any case, doing so and sending it to a prostitute in a small box and his general anti-social behavior in the small city of Arles prompted the townsfolk to lock him up in the insane asylum at nearby Saint Rémy. Sometime later, during his recovery, he asked permission to leave for the day to paint in the countryside. Earlier, during his time in Arles, it wasn't unusual for him to spend hours each day struggling with 'Plein air' painting, his easel staked to the ground and his canvases tied to the easel to prevent the mistrals from toppling everything over. In this case, as he was mostly recovered, the asylum allowed him a day pass. During this long afternoon of painting, the winds came up quite fiercely. Later that evening, Van Gogh became distraught and set about drinking his painting turpentine.

I rather doubt Vincent's suicide can be attributable to any single event. Yet, I find compelling the poetic imagery imbued in the possibility of the artist dismantled by the winds. It isn't a great leap of the imagination to see the mistrals appear in the paintings he painted while in Arles-the swirling energy found in the application of pigment as if he could hear the unhearable as anything he could see before him. Did he sense the destructive forces of the winds? I'm sure he did. The poignant irony is that he tried to cut off the organ that helps sound enter the brain and shape our mental perceptions.

When Vincent was released from the asylum and left the south of France, he went to Auvers-sur-Oise, twenty-seven kilometers northwest of Paris, and was somewhat under the care of Doctor Gachet. Within months after arriving, it is generally held that Vincent went to a small wooden shed, shot himself in the heart, collapsed, revived, and returned to the Ravoux home, where he boarded. He died the following day. The daughter of Monsieur Ravoux, Adeline Ravoux, who was twelve years old, wrote an account of the event some years later. However, buried in the original letters, it indicates that he shot himself in the groin. How can this be reconciled? One plausible explanation: the date, 1890, was during the final decade of the Victorian era, a period of such enormous prudishness that even pianos could not be said to have legs. Anything sexual or having to do with certain body parts was immensely taboo. It's more than likely, if Vincent's wound had been in the groin, this would not have been discussed or divulged to the general public and certainly not to a twelve-year-old girl. According to Vincent's statement, once revived from shooting himself, he tried to find the gun to finish the job but could not, and no one could find the weapon. In her accounting, Adeline suggested that Vincent did not commit suicide; someone shot him. But who?

Even without medical knowledge, one could easily suppose that a man shot in the groin might survive longer than had he been shot in the heart, and had he intended the heart, he must have missed by some degree. If we assume it was a wound in the groin, we can only wonder why there, whether self-inflicted or not. It took over thirty-seven hours for him to die in extreme pain.

There has long been a belief by many that Van Gogh was homosexual. While there is no evidence to prove this, there is no evidence to disprove it. We do know that he was enormously fascinated with fellow painter Paul Gauguin. After he left Arles, Gauguin wrote to a friend that he woke in the middle of the night on two occasions to find Vincent standing above his bed staring at him. When Gauguin asked what he was doing, Vincent turned and fled from Gauguin's bedroom in a panic.

In her account, Adeline writes, "That Sunday, he went out immediately after lunch, which was unusual. At dusk, he had not returned, which surprised us very much, for he was extremely correct in his relationship with us; he always kept regular meal hours. We were then all sitting out on the cafe terrace, for on Sunday, the hustle was more tiring than on weekdays. When we saw Vincent arrive, night had fallen; it must have been about nine o'clock. Vincent walked bent, holding his stomach, again exaggerating his habit of holding one shoulder higher than the other. Mother asked him: "M. Vincent, we were anxious. We are happy to see you return; have you had a problem?"

He replied in a suffering voice: "No, but I have..." He did not finish. He crossed the hall, took the staircase, and climbed to his bedroom. I was witness to this scene. Vincent made such a strange impression that Father got up and went to the stairs to see if he could hear anything.

He thought he could hear groans, went up quickly, and found Vincent on his bed, laid down in a crooked position, knees up to the chin, moaning loudly: " What's the matter, "said Father," are you ill? Vincent then lifted his shirt and showed him a small wound in the region of the heart. Father cried:

"Malheureaux, [unhappy man], what have you done?"

"I have tried to kill myself," replied Van Gogh.

These words are precise; our father retold them many times to my sister and me. And I, because for our family, the tragic death of Vincent Van Gogh has remained one of the most prominent events of our life. In his old age, Father became blind and gladly aired his memories, and the suicide of Vincent was the one that he told the most often and with great precision."

Clearly, the young girl saw Vincent come in, bent over, holding his stomach and in great pain, but she did not accompany her father to the bedroom and only relied on her father's words about the location of the bullet wound.

Thus history has recorded it.

Many years after Vincent's death, fascinating revelations appeared. During Vincent's time in Auvers-sur-Oise, hiking through the country-side with his easel and paint box, he was considered quite eccentric. That June 1890, a group of young boys in their late teens from wealthy families vacationed in the area and delighted in tormenting Vincent, often buying him alcohol to fuel their fun. One recalled decades later that they had seen Vincent in and about the villages and teased him, admitting they had a gun they used for hunting. Could it all have been a sad accident, a prank gone awry? Not wanting the boys to suffer from criminal action, Vincent claimed he attempted suicide. Possible? Yes.

Here remains an untold and unsolvable mystery. Did Vincente take his own life, or did someone murder him? We have no idea where he went, who Vincent might have seen, or under what circumstances. As it stands in history, all of this—his neural highway shattered from infrason-ic sound waves and his sexual coding—might mean little in the shadow of his monumental genius and what he left us. On the other hand, it does not harm to muse upon any mystery nor the possibility that Vincent ended his life because he could not find a way to express what is most fundamental in human nature—his sexual identity.

Societies and their cultural skins have changed remarkably in some ways from the prurient age of Queen Victoria. The 20th century ushered in radical changes, such as nuclear weapons, television, fast food, and the great sexual revolution I witnessed in the 1960s. Many of us believed that out of these winds of change, a paradigm would rise, something more lasting with a greater understanding of the fantastic panoply of human-ity with a greater tolerance for racial differences, religious and non-reli-gious beliefs, and sexual expressions. What came seems short-lived.

Many young people have committed suicide in the last few years, and many suffer from brutal teasing and physical abuse. The sexual blueprint of these children is given to them by the grace of nature, yet some choose death rather than suffer unwarranted shame from the pain of our ignorance and intolerance. Are we doomed to devolve? Our cultural trajectory is never linear and seems weighted by anxiety, doubt, and fear; history reveals how mythical are men's wings.

Whenever the winds come up, I cannot but think of Vincent toiling in his solitude beneath the intense sun of Southern France. What might his paintings have looked like had he not gone south, and how many immeasurable gifts might he have left us had he not left this world at such a young age? He was thirty-seven.

November 21, 2010

Lean Out into the World

I don't know about you, but when I stick my head out into the winds of American political discourse, I not only get a queasy, noxious feeling, as though something once loved has died unloved, but I also feel as though everything is moving backward more rapidly than forward. How have we come so far and yet seem to be regressing to the point where the pursuit of witches will be the next item discussed by various factions of those meant to be tending to the government? Take, for example, the issue of same-sex marriage that still occupies so much political real estate when the more significant concerns should be about our dismal attention to climate, financial collapse, and human greed that achieved it. The central reasoning against same-sex marriage is couched within religion, espousing that marriage is a 'sacred institution between a man and a woman. I'm not at all clear what modern American fundamentalists or conservative politicians mean by 'sacred institution' since, for the most significant part of human history up until the most recent of times, women, by and large, have had very little say in who is to be their husband and were generally treated as chattel. In many parts of the world, this situation still exists. What could be sacred about slavery? It's hardly surprising that most politicians, bishops, ministers, preachers of the gospel, popes, rabbis, mullahs, writers of Christian, Islamic, Hindu, and Buddhist scripture, and dictators were and are men, not to mention the gender of most religion's primary deity.

What is also never mentioned in these proclamations about the sanctity of marriage is that nearly fifty percent of marriages in the United States end in divorce; this percentage continues to rise. Additionally, an equally large portion of children is born out of wedlock. Data from the National Center for Health Statistics showed, in 2007, forty percent of babies born in the US were delivered from unwed mothers.

The current arguments against same-sex marriage, the 'Don't Ask, Don't Tell policy, and gay rights, are generally driven not so much by religious institutions but by political deviousness. Indeed, not for the first time in history has this obfuscating shell game been played. While technologies change and cultures shift, deception is, and always has been, pretty much the same. The extreme wealthy (individuals, corporations, and policy institutions) pay politicians to pander to the public's lack of knowledge and stoke the fires of fear. A perfect smokescreen rises, almost always under the guise of religion but devoid of fundamental ethics.

Gay issues are the perfect foil for this irredeemable power-hungry system because same-sex desire remains the least understood human complexity. Even though there is abundant scientific evidence supporting homosexuality as a naturally occurring expression, many people, especially religious conservatives, believe that gays choose to be gay; therefore, they can change. Such are the beliefs and proclamations of the husband of one of the current Presidential contenders, who has made a business-reparative therapy out of converting gays to straights. Presumably, it is her conviction as well. It is incredible and terrifying that this kind of voodoo rubbish can prevail anywhere within miles of the slightest bit of intelligence, let alone at this level of political discourse.

The notion of choice is predicated on the Biblically historical belief that humans are the beneficiaries of 'free will' while non-humans are not, presumably because we became too smart for our own good. There is abundant scientific evidence supporting the contrary; over 1500 species participate in various levels of homosexual activity.

It is politically effective to convert everything to black or white, and conventional media adds to the confusion with its obscure filters. There is no absolute 'state' in human sexuality, and there never has been. There is black, and there is white. But in between, there exist uncountable greys.

If a gay person is homosexual by choice, we must assume heterosexuals are likewise straight because they choose to be. If this is so, all heterosexuals are capable of having same-sex desires, as are homosexuals. Can this be? Unlikely. More likely, a percentage of heterosexuals never experience same-sex desire. On the opposite side of the spectrum are those with no desire for the opposite sex.

Between the two, there is a remarkable gradation from one to the other. Pansexuality is an indivisible fabric of grays, blacks, and whites woven from genetic predisposition but immensely pressed upon by cultural weight. Human sexuality is complicated, complex, and rich in diversity.

Millions of individuals marry, have children, then decide to 'come out,' choosing to express their natural state of same-sex desire. 'Coming out is a choice, divorce is a choice, cruelty is a choice, intolerance is a choice, greed is a choice, and bigotry is a choice. Same-sex desire is not a choice. It is a state of being. It is neither right nor wrong; it simply is. The less attention we pay to those who claim otherwise, the better off we'll be. As poet and filmmaker James Broughton once said, "Don't pollute the Divine with religion; it takes all the fresh air out of Paradise."

November 13, 2011

God The Water—The Ethics Of Goodness

The other day I went to the currency exchange window at my local bank in Chiang Mai. In front of me was a young American completing a money exchange, converting US dollars to Thai currency. He was neatly dressed in a crisp white shirt, dark slacks, and a green silk tie that shimmered beneath the rosy glow of his clean-shaven, Nordic face. Apparently, in the exchange, the teller had accidentally overpaid him. The customer, having caught the mistake, returned the money.

I arrived as the teller was gratefully thanking him. The young man replied, "I returned the money because I'm a Christian. God bless you." He smiled and then disappeared into a bright, steamy afternoon.

I suspect the young acolyte's missionary fervor obscured any sense of his offense. The Thai bank teller, who might have been a Christian, was likely a Buddhist since Thailand is over ninety percent Buddhist. But the point remains that the young American's comment was insulting, and he implied that Christians are honest and morally steadfast while those practicing Judaism, Sikhism, Jainism, Animism, Confucianism, and Buddhism are not. Those who are Taoists, Hindus, and atheists are not.

Many Christians believe that if you don't accept Christ as your personal Savior, you don't have a prayer of getting into heaven. Their god is 'The' God, and that is that. If you're not a Christian but want to reap the benefits of eternal salvation, you must be redeemed by a miraculous Christian epiphany or a transfiguration within the Word.

Imagine an undiscovered island where a group of happy folk lived. They have no written language, but almost everybody remembers everything said. The children were taught not to kill one another, lie or steal, or covet other people's property. They were instructed to obey and respect their elders and work for the community's benefit. The boys were taught to respect mothers, sisters, and wives as different but equal components in the fabric of their lives, and the people taught each other to respect the spirit of all living and non-living things. After several millennia, they settled on a god. They called their god Water. The people were healthy and happy, and Water replenished their needs. They were surrounded by their god and bathed in their god; they drank daily of their god; their crops flourished, and their children seeded and bloomed in the god of the womb.

One day a foreign ship landed on the shores. Out of it poured an army of Christians. Their first objective was to bring the island's people into the bosom of Christ and to the Word of their God. To the soldiers of the cross, it hardly mattered that the moral framework of the people who believed in Water was no different than that espoused by Christians. This belief is like the teacher saying to his students, "I don't care if you have all the right answers. I'll flunk you anyway because you didn't learn them from me."

A few months ago, I traveled up into the hill tribe country of Northern Thailand to visit my Akha friends. The Akha are among many hill tribes living in Northern Thailand, Burma, Laos, and China. Their traditional religion is Animism, a primitive belief system in which animate and inanimate objects are imbued with an innate soul. Rice and where it's planted is high on their list of life's essentials.

I can't deny that Christian missionaries have often assisted in the endless plight of hill tribe communities, but usually at some cost and diminishment of culture and spirit. The least of which is bribery. "I'll give you money, medicine, and hope if you believe in my god. Who cares about yours?" The worst bears remembering. The atrocities of murder and genocide, enslavement and torture, under the name and bloody banner of the Christian Church, are too numerous to count and too horrific to fathom.

Sadly, most havoc, promulgated by religious zealotry, is initially dispensed by the few who use religion as a palliative to seduce the many into wars for the perpetuation of personal power and wealth. When the founders of American Democracy felt it imperative to separate Church and State, they knew very well the beneficial qualities of human actions are intrinsic, irrespective of our gods. Morality is not a residual benefit of any religion; it is the only trait we possess that allows us to co-exist with one another. As a species, that's something to consider and something to nurture. Today, more than ever, we should all be careful and ever-vigilant. Greed is constantly unweaving the fabric of democracy, and the cloak of religion is descending into something rather dark and menacing.

We don't know what Jesus or Buddha said millennia ago; we only know how others later explained their thoughts. Knowledge is merely a set of interpretations we've inherited. If we could take all the religions in this world, put them in a big kettle, and render them to a rare viscosity, the results would be everyday goodness and a thick aftertaste of reasonableness.

The young man at the bank returned the money, not because he was a Christian or Buddhist, but simply because it was the right thing to do.

October 12, 2010

Morris Graves, *Northwest Mystic Painter*

Despite a prodigious creative output spanning six decades and is universally celebrated as one of the most influential American painters of 20th-century modern art, Morris Graves, who died in 2001, not only remains an enigma but is relatively unknown, especially to younger generations. This loss is partly attributable to the fact that Graves himself retreated from the public stage; he eschewed fame. He believed that his artistic contribution had significance only as part of a larger vessel of creative visionary expression.

So it is not surprising that throughout his life, he chose not to attend the openings of his exhibitions. Even as Graves continued to retreat into his beloved privacy, constructing his homes and gardens and making art, the extraverted world of abstract expressionism exploded in New York with bolder, brighter, and bigger images and celebrity-seeking creators, all antipodal to the contemplative, visionary world Graves inhabited.

Graves was a true visionary, a painter who sought that which is eternal. But the search was not without conflict. The burgeoning encroachment of industry and the machines and mentality of human conflict continued to invade Graves' habitats. He continually sought out places of solitude in the United States and Ireland, finally establishing a remote habitat hidden in the ancient forests of Northern California. His path as a "solitary romantic" from which he breathed in the communion of life's ineffable essence was one of natural wonder. From within his gardens, the universe spoke. The inhabitants—small animals, birds, and flora—fed his emplastic powers of cognition, the unifying gift of the imagination.

I recently conversed with an artist who, a decade earlier, had received her bachelor's degree in art from a credible New York University. When I mentioned the name Morris Graves, she appeared perplexed. She thought the name vaguely familiar but had no idea when or where he had lived and knew nothing about his work. Morris Cole Graves, born in Fox Valley, Oregon, in 1910, was a self-taught artist who became, next to Mark Tobey, an essential visionary artist of the Northwest School. In the early 1940s, Graves' work was selected as part of New York's Museum of Modern Art's "Americas

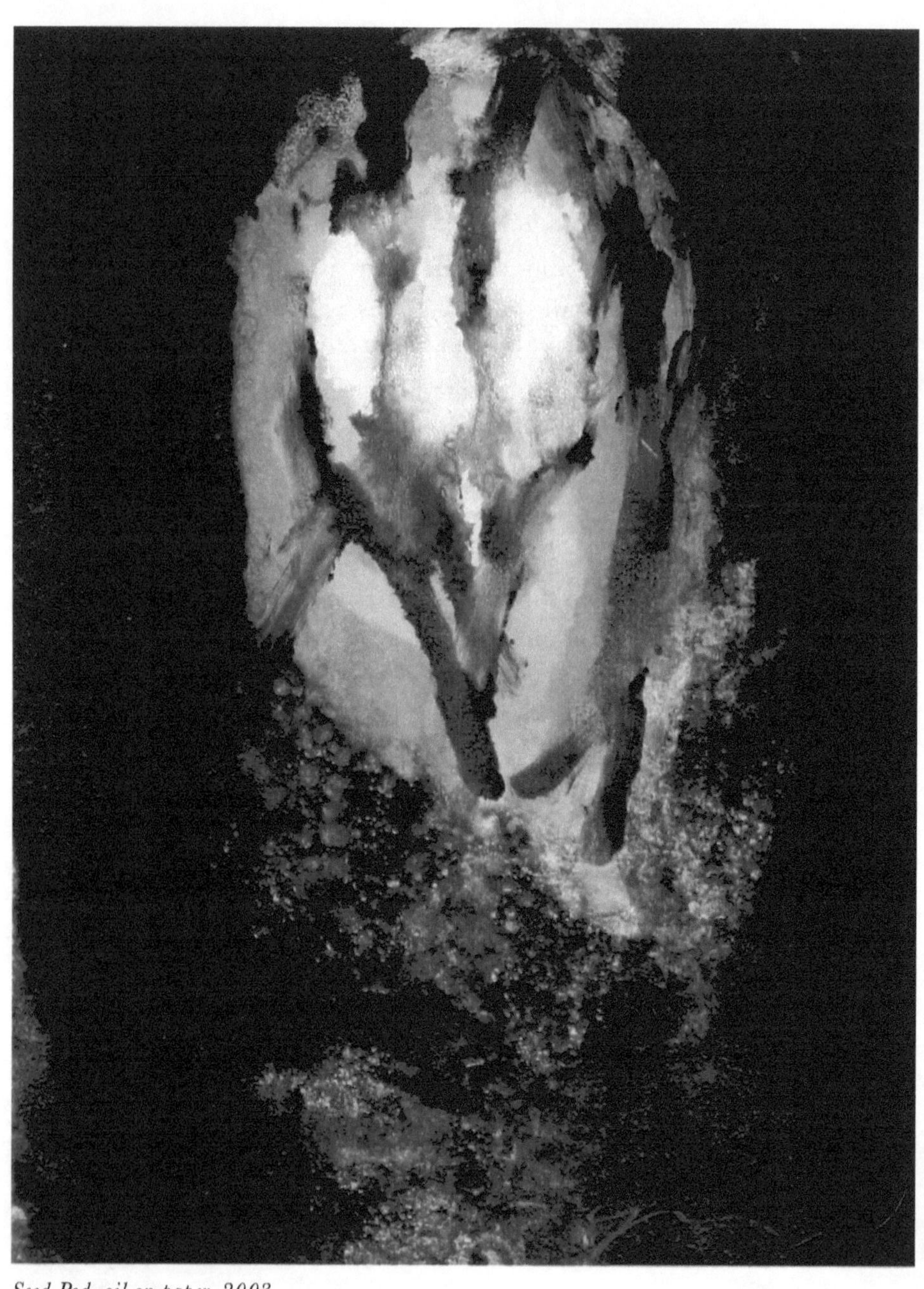

Seed Pod, oil on paper, 2003

1942". This event catapulted him into international recognition. Even so, Graves continued to retreat into his beloved privacy, constructing his homes and gardens and making art. At the same time, the extraverted world of abstract expressionism exploded in New York with bolder, brighter images, all antipodal to the contemplative, visionary world Graves inhabited.

During the Second World War, Graves spent time in a military prison as a conscientious objector. From these early anti-war sentiments evolved his deep interest in and exploration of the philosophies of the Far East, an amalgam of Hinduism, Taoism, and Zen Buddhism-all human constructs, nonetheless reflective of his thoughts on the universality and the singularity of nature, the wondrousness of the 'Way.' Graves's imagery was considered unique, but his reasons for making the art were not; they were ancient. For Graves, his animals and flowers represented inner visions of the unconscious, the Atman, symbolic of the potential "self."

When Morris Graves began his flower paintings of the early seventies, a few critics suggested he had lost his great visual power. They accused him of painting only 'pretty flowers.' It no doubt amused him that that was all they saw. Graves' ability to make evident the unity of the spirit through paint is present in these later works. His form relationships and the inherent interstices, the subtle migration of hues within a single blossom, are things we talk about. But not the inexplicable "pneuma." We refer to the painting the way a title refers to the painting and, in fact, the way the painting merely refers to a generative and immutable, creative spirit. The gift is not the painting but the artist's accrued love and generosity from the making of it. The painting as object is simply a map for the soul.

2010 marks the centennial year of this remarkable artist. He is no longer here, but through his paintings, his great longing and love for the ineffable still resonate, binding us one to another.

October 9th, 2010

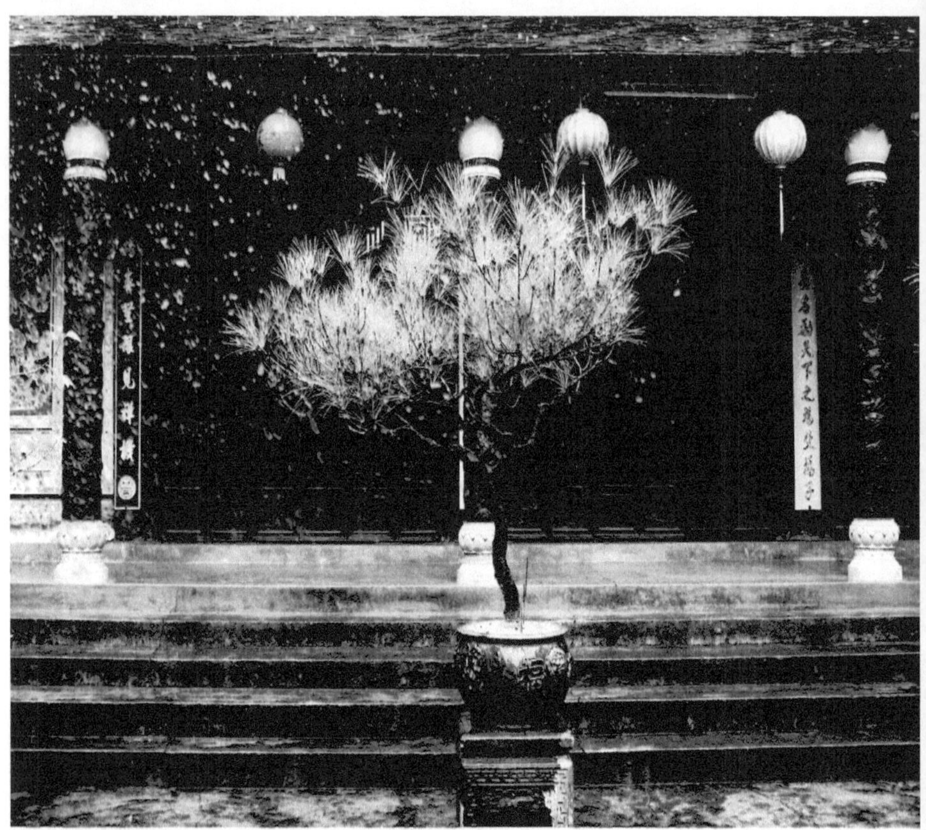

Temple at Thich Nhat Hanh Retreat, Vietnam, photograph, 2014

Small Footprints, Big Journeys

One hundred and nine kilometers northwest of Chiangmai, perched on this side of the border between Thailand and what is officially called Myanmar, formerly known (And still called by many) as Burma, lies the district of Wiang Haeng, within which is a collection of small villages not on the typical tourist route. I drove across a green sea of rice fields from Chiangmai, then up and down the nearly vertical mountains that rise majestically from the plains. I was on a journey to learn more about a remarkable group of young Buddhist novices and nains, the latter being young children to young adults. The age for being ordained a Thai monk is twenty. In July, this group of devoted young men won a collective UNAID Red Ribbon Award at the AIDS 2010 Ceremony in Vienna, Austria, for their exceptional community service.

Like most people in this area, these young Buddhists have come from the Shan State, across the border from Wiang Haeng. The history of the Shan, a Tai ethnic group, is complicated, and their political relationships with neighboring groups are even more convoluted. In 2001, border conflicts erupted between the Shan and the Wa. The Wa people have agreed to trade their autonomy for support from the military regime of the Union of Myanmar. by helping destabilize the Shan State through encroachment on Shan territories. A primary goal of the Myanmar junta is to eliminate the Shan State, both culturally and politically, and they have been ruthless in their methods.

During the conflicts between the Shan and the WA, the Myanmar army moved in swiftly, destroying village after village, families torn apart; in many cases, children witnessed their parents being tortured and murdered and their mothers raped by army soldiers. Thousands managed to escape across the border into Thailand, where they remain. However, even today, many are not afforded official refugee status but are simply stateless people struggling in poverty.

I visited Phratyhat Wat Fa Wiang In, a temple that had once been entirely on Thai soil but now is severed in half by new boundaries due to the 2001 conflict. Separated by only several hundred feet, across a pastoral gully planted with fruit trees and deadly land mines, we stared at what used to be dormitories for Thai monks; the army now uses them as barracks. On the Thai side, young nains and a few novices busily sweep up leaves near the main chedi. We spoke with a Shan monk who had secretly crossed back into Burma with a camera hidden beneath his robs. For weeks he traveled his country, copying old Shan photographs and documents hidden from the junta. Had he been caught, the consequences would have been certain imprisonment or death. Another group of older novices was busy with whatever primitive tools they could find to remodel an old temple building to house this collection of historical artifacts. It will be a museum to help preserve the culture of the Shan people.

The results of this devastating conflict brought numerous and immediate problems-Smuggling methamphetamine pills, known as yaba. This year alone, 400,000 pills have been confiscated in only one seizure. It's rumored that corrupt groups within the WA State Army of Myanmar bring in most illegal drugs. Like so much of the world, populations struggling in poverty, hopelessness, and desperation are prey to these crippling drugs. The intensity of delivery and increasing addictive strength of yaba continue to grow, supplying an endless demand. Equally devastating are the social scars from the sex-trade industry. Some girls and young women are sold as sex slaves and smuggled into Thai brothels, while some, both women and young men, volunteer out of desperation to help support their families. It's all too obvious what lies on the other side of this sad equation-a dangerous and demoralizing rise in the HIV/AIDS epidemic and drug addiction.

In his re-adaptation of the "Tibetan Wheel of Dependent Origination" to the problems of HIV/AIDS, Buddhist, teacher, and humanitarian, Lawrence Maund articulates the chain of events that originate from ignorance. There follows fear, then discrimination and segregation. This path of darkness leads to unemployment, loss of income, financial worries, stress and anxiety, depression, hopelessness, and withdrawal. We neglect our mental and physical health, falling into sickness, despair, and death.

Under the guidance of senior monk and educator Phra Thanee, these are the problems the novices and nains are tackling. From various temples throughout the area, they have come to a center they call Pleekawiwek (a place of peaceful solitude suitable for meditation). Their purpose is to learn everything they can about the effects on their communities from HIV/AIDS and drug addiction and the positive ways they can disseminate that learning back into the villages. What is of primary concern is to eliminate the stigma of HIV/AIDS that has, through ignorance, attached itself in the minds of the people, for those who carry the virus and those who do not; everyone is affected.

This understanding and teaching are relegated to more than just these problems. What has grown from this benevolence is a holistic approach from which seeds of hope and recourse sprout - the development and use of organic fertilizers and pesticides. They also teach the people how to make inexpensive mud-brick houses for themselves and instruct villagers on the positive elements of life skills. A small group of energetic spirits dedicates their lives to making a difference for those in need.

Pleekawiwek is a quiet, peaceful place yet charged with energy from these young Buddhists, moving and with utter conviction, changing the world step by step. It is a small footprint but a compelling journey with big rewards. In the pulse of their hearts, their actions move on the river of Buddhist thought, "Neither fire nor wind, birth nor death can erase our good deeds."

We live in a time of much distress in the world; the creative richness of individual spirits flounders by a dark cloud of capitalism and corporatism. We are suffocating from consumerism and greed. Such illness cannot be healed from the large to the small, only from the small to the large.

I believe the spirit of Pleekawiwek is this kind of extraordinary gift, from the few to the many, through which we can begin to heal from the loss of something found neither in governments nor religions but in fundamental, natural, positive goodness given to us from this earth.

October 29, 2010

Ed and Ed

Monday, September 10, 2001

It was mid-afternoon when I drove out to visit my friend, Ed Cain, on his five-acre parcel of land near Port Townsend, Washington. In a clearing of Douglas fir and white cedar, he'd built a modest two-room house and studio, a sizable vegetable garden, and several large pens in which he kept his prized chickens.

Ed had been married twice, with children from both marriages, and even though his second family lived on the opposite corner of the acreage in a house he'd built for them, he preferred his solitude. He lived alone.

He greeted me at the door with his usual good nature. "Get on in here," he said, sweeping his right arm down and out into the room as if to say, "OK, you found me." Ten feet into the room, we stopped and stood before one of his newest paintings, a large silver and black abstraction that nearly filled one wall. I smiled and nodded appreciatively. Then he led me across the room, around an old platen press, through his kitchen, and out the back door to a small porch where we settled into a lengthy conversation. Trees towered above us on all sides.

We hadn't seen each other in several weeks and, as usual, were soon discussing our inescapable, irresistible tether to art, the joy we found in making it, and the various ways it entered and affected our lives. Our newest topic, however, was Ed's participation in several of my film projects.

Some months earlier, I'd interviewed him for "Cadmium Red Light," a documentary profile of Lennie Kesl, an eccentric painter and jazz singer who had been my friend and mentor for nearly forty years. In the mid-1980s, I'd introduced both men, and they quickly bonded; it seemed fitting that Ed should add his two cents to the project's rich collection of interviews.

Ed was happy to do so. But what he ultimately offered surprised me. A different person emerged—not the gentle Ed I'd expected but an off-the-wall, slightly cantankerous character with sharp-edged humor. I was fascinated with what whirled out of his imagination, and

I immediately sensed another project blossoming. I asked him if he would let me continue the interviews, not about Lennie, but about himself or whichever "self" appeared.

What developed in this new project was a delightful fable. Ed, or Edward, split himself into fictitious identical twins: Edward and Edwin. In the reeling out of his entwining yarn, Edward was serious and artistic, Edwin cranky and countrified, a man who loved his chickens.

Being interviewed first, Edward explained that family tradition dictated the first-born son was to be named Edward. When the twin boys arrived, their parents decided to call one Edward and the other Edwin. Until they were older, they were simply known as the little 'Eddys.'

"OK," I said, smiling, "I'm game. Let's see where the story drifts."

Edward continued. He explained that Edwin had fallen off a horse while trying to jump over a feed trough, landing on his head. My brother was a bit slow. After their mother died, Edward took his brother in, allowing him to help around the yard, tend the chickens, and weed the garden to keep him busy and out of trouble.

When I interviewed Edwin, however, the story changed. In this slant, it was Edwin who took care of Edward.

"Edward," Edwin complained, "ain't good for much. He can't make a living. He don't do nothing but write poetry. He never did. And those pictures? Hell, nobody can understand them things. If he'd get himself a decent job, he might do OK. I've been taking care of him since Mom passed."

On the surface, this unfolding invention seemed like a delightful comedy, but it was also unsettling in its 'believability.' I couldn't quite put my finger on it.

After four or five interviews, the film's title, conjured up by Edwin, asserted itself. It would be called "Ed and Ed."

Of course, the Ed Cain I had known for eighteen years had no twin. He had grown up in the American West, part cowboy, part farmer, and eventually, he tried his hand as a chef, a landscaper, and at general construction. Ed was a competent plumber and electrician—a true jack of all trades. He even dug his own well with muscle and shovel.

Ed was also a remarkable poet and painter. He designed and handset the type for his limited edition books and printed them on that old printing press he had dragged around for years. His poetry is sparse and elegant. His paintings are figurative abstractions of birds-mostly loons and crows or the human female, often expressed in bold, child-like strokes of black and white.

Ed was a big, tall man who spoke quietly and possessed a gentle, generous heart. He loved to tease his way through conversations, always making you comfortable. Our conversation migrated from art in general to the specifics of setting up our next interview session.

As the afternoon passed, the sun had moved beyond the clearing, and the air grew colder. Ed's light bantering slowed, and his usual bright disposition darkened. He seemed to slowly collapse in on himself as he leaned both arms on the table, clearing his throat as one might do when wanting to change the subject. He paused, looked over the table at me, and softly asked, "What do you think I should do with my work... with my paintings?"

"What do you mean?" I replied.

"Well, I don't think anyone much cares about them one way or the other," he said, looking down at his large hands clasped together, fingers twisting in fingers as if in agitated prayer. "I thought you might have some ideas."

I looked at my friend, disturbed by what he was asking. However, I didn't take his question too seriously because, while generous to a fault with his friends, Ed was perhaps the most independent, self-reliant person I'd ever met. Returning a favor always required subtle ingenuity. I stuttered for an appropriate response until my awkwardness left a lengthy gap in our conversation. He felt my discomfort and quickly lightened the mood.

We stood and wandered back inside, through the kitchen, around the press, and toward the front door.

I explained that I would leave for Thailand within a week to resume work on my elephant documentary. I told him I would consider his question and offer the best advice before leaving the country. I suggested I return in a few days to get more material for "Ed and Ed." I was excited by what we had, but we both agreed it wasn't enough.

He smiled broadly beneath his thick mustache and walked me to the door, switching on his 'Edwinesque' humor. We laughed and shook hands. I got into my car and drove home.

* * * * *

On Wednesday, like almost every other person in the world, I was still staggering from Tuesday's unimaginable destruction: planes crashing into the World Trade Center, bodies burning or falling from those iconic buildings, another plane crashing into the Pentagon, and yet another plunging into the wooded fields near 'Shanksville,' Pennsylvania.

No one had ever witnessed anything like it on American soil since the bombing of Pearl Harbor. 9/11 was a catastrophic event that irrevocably changed how we think and act as a culture; it spawned an entirely new matrix of fear-technology, governmental invasion of privacy, unreasonable wars, and systemic hatred.

I received a phone call from Ed's estranged wife that early evening. She was in Oregon, traveling up to Port Townsend. She had been trying to reach Ed but without success. When she returned the following day, having to go directly to her office, she phoned me again, still concerned, and asked if I would check on him.

"OK," I told her, "I'll drive out."

I tried his phone. No answer. So I drove the five miles back out Hastings Avenue, down Jolie Way onto his long, unpaved driveway through the fir trees, until I reached his house.

I found myself crafting a rather dark what-if scenario as I drove to his home. I don't believe my turn of thoughts came from any feeling I left with after seeing him on Monday but rather from being emotionally troubled by the disaster of 9/11.

If Ed planned to do something to himself, he would destroy all his chickens first. It was odd to imagine, but that was where my mind turned. Everything would be fine if I heard his chickens as I approached the house, and if I heard nothing, I should worry.

When I arrived, I saw his white van parked in its usual place. The front door to his house was open. I rolled down my window and listened. Silence. My heart raced a bit. Then I heard a few hens and a squabbling rooster. I felt reassured. I got out, stood by my car, and called his name several times. No response. I called a bit louder. Still nothing. It was a lovely, clear, sunny September morning with a slight breeze.

I walked up and stood at the bottom of his front porch. "Hey, Ed, are you there...are you inside?" The chickens started fussing; they were hungry.

I heard a voice coming from the interior. But it wasn't Ed's. It sounded as if it were coming from a TV. Then it hit me; I suddenly realized what I was about to walk into. Though reluctant to step inside, I entered because I had no choice. "Just go in," I said aloud, praying I wouldn't find what I was afraid I might.

Entering, I saw dead leaves had blown into the room and were scattered about in small drifts across the floor. Between Ed's front door and kitchen, the printing press stood in quiet obstinacy, waiting for the next book project to begin.

Little clay sculptures of diving birds lined the shelf beneath the windows. The large painting I'd seen on Monday loomed more intensely, the black and silver paint piercing the room's dark interior from sunlight flooding through the open door.

I turned slowly to the right. Ed's body lay on what seemed too small of a bed, his shoulders propped up on several pillows. He wore only a white undershirt that had gathered and risen above his stomach. A rifle lay near his side, his right hand curled over the stock.

A small portable TV sat on a crate beside his bed; it seemed like some strange intensive care device, noisily attending the body that lay before it. The bullet had entered through his mouth, exiting the upper back of his head. The force of the projectile had exploded the skull's parietal bone and left a large, irregular pattern of blood and flesh against the wall. Yet his face was strangely tranquil, as if he were merely in repose, eyes shut, calmly listening to the newscast. I stood transfixed in the aftermath of mayhem—the strange juxtaposition between Ed's lifeless body and the television's low droning, its constant spooling out of tragedy into the world.

I had entered a new experience, operating autonomously as if by script. I found Ed's phone. It was on a table beneath the window that looked out into the yard. I knew I needed to dial 911, but first, I called a friend, another artist.

"Call Stephen," I said. "Please ask him to come over."

Then I dialed the emergency operator. I looked out of the window into the yard. I remember thinking how beautiful and green was his vegetable garden. I could hear the clucking and crooning of chickens. "I need to report a suicide," I told the operator.

"Are you certain he's dead?"

"Yes, I'm sure of it. He's dead."

"How far are you from the body?"

"I'm close... maybe fifteen feet. It's... it's a small room."

"Can you take the phone into another room?"

"No, I can't."

"OK. But I need you to stay on the line. Keep talking to me. Stay on the line. The sheriff is on his way. He should be there soon."

"This is very difficult."

"I know it is, sir, but I need you to stay on the line."

After the initial shock—the mind's processing of death, a friend's death, of seeing what the force of a bullet does to flesh and bone, and of seeing his nearly naked body slumped against the wall on which his last creative expression was painted in blood—I turned away.

My being overwhelmed released some chemicals that helped me defy my frailty. The body mercifully does that. I felt emotionally disconnected from what lay before me. As I waited for the sheriff to arrive, I held the phone to my ear, my eyes wandering everywhere but to the bed.

"Yes, I'm still here," I kept repeating, assuring the voice on the other end of the line.

On the windowsills and tables, lottery tickets had been scratched and tossed. Bills lay unopened. On a bedside table, a wine bottle stood empty. A dark-red upholstered chair lay on its side between the bed and a nearby closet. Just beyond the chair, a closet door stood open.

I doubt an autopsy was ever performed on Ed's body, and there is no way to be sure exactly when he pulled the trigger. But during my wait and to help me refrain from bolting, which I had thought I might, I began to imagine his final moments.

I set the scene: A man is lying on a small bed, trying to swim out of darkness, desperate to ease a sorrow he cannot name. His entire world is sinking, and a voice on TV confirms it. He makes a final decision. End it all. He must do it. Now. No hesitating. He rises and stumbles toward the closet, where he keeps his gun. He trips and knocks over the chair in his wobbling, drunken haste. He reaches into the closet, grabs the rifle, and returns to the bed. Don't think. Don't think. He pulls the trigger.

"Are you still with me?"

"Yes, I'm still here."

"The sheriff is heading up to the house now."

"I'm here."

"OK, now listen very carefully... what I need you to do, sir, is slowly put the phone down. Place it on the table, OK? Then I want you to calmly and slowly walk outside with both hands above your head. Do you understand?"

I did. I got it. Completely. Instantly. There was never a moment of indignant disbelief. I knew uncertainty surrounded me; I could have been the shooter.

I walked out calmly with my arms raised. The sheriff approached warily, obviously trying to get a read on any possible and unpredictable move I might make. I thought I heard him say, "It's OK." I relaxed and let my hands down. Quickly he reached for his holstered weapon.

Back up went my arms.

The county prosecuting attorney soon arrived; we'd known each for a few years. "He's OK," she said, moving between the sheriff and me, on into the house. The sheriff followed her inside, and an emergency vehicle arrived after a few more minutes. Two paramedics rolled out a gurney, and they went inside.

Ed's wife and son suddenly appeared from behind me, utter horror and disbelief on their faces.

They wanted to see Ed. I knew this could have devastating consequences, especially for the boy, so I forbade them.

"Go home," I said. "You do not want to see this."

Reluctantly they turned and left.

After a few minutes, the sheriff and county prosecutor departed the scene. The medics soon followed with Ed encased in a black body bag on the silver gurney. They placed him inside the emergency vehicle and slowly drove away.

No bright yellow tapes cordoned off the house. The sheriff had given me no instructions, and I stood in the yard stunned by the unfolding scenario, wondering what to do next. I assumed the county officials considered Ed's death self-inflicted and that they expected me to depart as everyone else had. But how could I? How could I leave the house open and unattended?

I went back inside. Ed was gone, the rifle gone, the television switched off, the house silent.

I knew I couldn't leave this place of pain and loss for the family to discover, so I searched Ed's kitchen for rags and cleaning supplies and began scrubbing the floor and the wall behind the bed. I drug the mattress into the yard, searched through Ed's studio, and found paint thinner to pour over it; I set it aflame.

Very soon, Stephen arrived, and we did our best to put the place back as if Ed were merely out for the afternoon. Stephen washed the dishes, and I put the empty wine bottle, stained towels, and bedding in plastic bags. We set the dark red chair upright, shut the closet door, then swept the dead leaves back into the yard. We closed the front door and left.

A week later, I headed back to Asia.

* * * * *

In November 2006, I finished "Cadmium Red Light" and had nearly completed the elephant documentary. I began to think about my scant video footage for "Ed and Ed."

The mini-tapes had lain undisturbed in their tiny, plastic box on a shelf in my office, gathering dust. I had not looked at the material since before Ed took his life.

But those three one-hour tapes always called to me.

As winter drove on, I began to feel like a six-penny nail orbiting Jupiter each time I went into my office, pulling me in; it was time to edit the twins.

Admittedly, I'd helped define the two characters by shaping my interviews to accommodate either Edward or Edwin.

Nonetheless, as I began to study the raw material, I wondered to what extent I had participated. Ed had orchestrated the entire scenario. It was his invention, his fable. "Ed and Ed" was his. I was merely shadowing his imagination.

I began to assemble what material I had. There wasn't much. I wanted to stay close to Ed's Ed, but I needed to understand why and I needed to know how. My job was to ensure the story would ultimately pass the honesty test. It did, after all, happen.

In one scene, Edward talks about bringing his brother to live with him after their parents died. He talks about going to 'Cenex,' a local garden store, to buy fertilizer for his vegetables.

When they have finished shopping and are back in the van, Edwin has a box of baby chicks on his lap. Edward says, "What do you have there?"

"Baby' Bafarmingtons,'" answers Edwin.

As far as I know, Ed never studied acting, yet he tells this simple fabrication with such conviction, his voice breaking, tears welling up in his eyes, that one cannot help but feel his brotherly love. It's a remarkable scene. as if he genuinely recalls some distant childhood memory.

As I struggled to develop a narrative, it soon became apparent that Edwin represented, in the real world of Ed Cain, everyone who couldn't understand him, his paintings, his poetry—his need to make art.

Edward suffered, in an inseparable way, the world of Edwin.

The challenge for me was weaving together a story with such limited material, achieving the necessary balance. It needed a beginning and an ending, and I wanted to ensure there was a purpose. And it also needed to be collaborative and what I imagined Ed would have liked. For the viewer and the integrity of the documentary, I had to finally stitch the brothers back together as one person, Ed Cain, to resolve it as history. Getting it there needed the right questions and answers.

After completing the first draft, I showed the film to several test groups. I needed feedback; I wanted to know whether I had created the illusion of actual twins and, more importantly, whether the fable transcended itself to become real. Would the film offer some lesson the viewer could grasp—a parable's gift?

Of the ten viewers, only one was uncertain, while the others fully believed they were watching identical twins until the ending when the two Eds were made one.

At the film's beginning, before Edwin appears, Edward reads one of his poems:

In winter one loon stays
just short of the farthest old piers.
Perhaps it is not always the same loon.

The light in this sun-diminished season
seems continual and it makes
little difference if it's dawn or evening.

In reflection, the loon seems not so cold.
The window mirrors my eyes against the haze.
The loon stills the air between us.

In the final scene, Edward sits on a metal stool near his platen press. As the interviewer, I explain that his brother Edwin has wholly dismissed his version of their life together. That Edwin had been taking care of him. Edward quietly laughs and says, "That's amazing. I'm surprised you got that much out of him. He usually doesn't talk that much. I don't know whether I want to dispute what he says."

He slowly stands, walks toward the viewer, and disappears. We are alone in the room with only the printing press and the little clay sculptures in the window. We see a message scrolling up and over the final scene. From these few words, we learn there was only Ed.

The viewer now understands the truth in the fable's revelation and the tragedy that befell Ed Cain.

In all probability, I was the last person to have seen him alive and the first to find what he'd left us. I would later ask myself, "Was I not listening well enough on that Monday afternoon? Was I overly concerned with my projects or my travel preparations?" Sadly, I missed any clues he might have given me that Monday.

Eight years later, however, going back through my last day of filming, I discovered in one sequence Edwin talking about their life together, his and Edward's. He says, "We don't have a desire to get involved with one another now." He adds, "It's almost 'door-shuttin' time.'" Does this unusual colloquialism refer merely to getting old and dying, or does it reveal darker thoughts? Ed was only sixty-six.

And was it possible, as Ed lay crippled in hopelessness, the news spewing out of the little TV became the proverbial straw that broke him beyond repair, another victim of 9/11?

It's been fourteen years since he asked me about his art and what will become of it. The question continues to haunt me. What can such a question mean?

He understood that the durability of art as an artifact is determined only by human capriciousness and the passage of time. But naturally and rightfully, he was concerned with what might become of his paintings and poems. Perhaps, for him, they tethered one world to another.

Ed and I often talked about the communion of art and how it nourishes and sustains generosity. We felt that the vitality of art is indelible and processional: conceiving, doing, and giving. We believed it then, and I believe it still.

When I think back on that Monday afternoon, as we sat across from one another beneath those magnificent trees, Ed wasn't asking me a question but offering an awkward and oblique farewell.

In the end, Ed left this world, Edwin's world, in solitude, and as he did so, like his beautiful loon, he stilled the air between us.

A War That Counts
Homelessness and Poverty in the United States

For a while now, a good friend of mine in Seattle has been sending me photographic portraits of homeless men and women he encounters around his small office in the Ballard area of the city. While the imagery cannot hide the dreariness of their situation, what my friend tries to convey in the portraits is a sense of commonality, a shared humanity. Most of us will cross the street to avoid confronting a homeless person, and we seldom wish to make eye contact with such a person whose circumstances of life terrify us for whatever reason. But my friend is an unusual individual, selfless and sensitive to the plights of others. He is not afraid to engage with the homeless, to inquire about their life, where they come from, and what might have been the circumstances that brought them such desolation, hunger, and an abject sense of being. To look deeply into the eyes of any of us, we find a bit of all of us. We cannot escape ourselves.

Like my friend, many know that such a preponderance of deprivation in our country represents a societal illness becoming increasingly difficult to ignore. In a way, the great 'State of Homeless' represents an entirely separate state; think of it as the fifty-first state, the boundaries of which extend westward beyond the State of California, eastward beyond the shores of the Atlantic Ocean, as far north as the Arctic circle, and as far south as the earth's equator. It is a landless state, seamlessly woven throughout all states, one of desperation, poverty, and hunger, with a population estimated roughly the same as the state of Connecticut's 3.5 million people. At any given time, slightly over ten percent of our population is homeless. And it grows. Of course, it's impossible to know the numbers or how many children go to bed hungry each night in this country.

Funding for programs designed to help America's poor and hungry are being cut when we pour money into a country with a population nearly identical to our 'State of Homeless.' Since the onset of the Libyan conflict, we have spent over half a billion dollars with an expected continuation of 40 million a month without any guarantee of an outcome other than it feeds the military-industrial complex and global corporate interests enormously. This figure pales compared to the money we've spent in Iraq and Afghanistan, with billions unaccounted for. It has been estimated that the money spent on these uncertain wars could have eradicated poverty and homelessness in the United States for the next century.

We would all do well to read, again and again, President Eisenhower's 1961 farewell speech. Equally important, as his warning about the danger of allowing the military-industrial complex (corporatism) to grow too large, are those words found in his closing paragraph. "We pray that peoples of all faiths, all races, all nations, may have their great human needs satisfied; that those now denied opportunity shall come to enjoy it to the full; that all who yearn for freedom may experience its spiritual blessings; that those who have freedom will understand, also, its heavy responsibilities; that all who are insensitive to the needs of others will learn charity; that the scourges of poverty, disease, and ignorance will be made to disappear from the earth, and that, in the goodness of time, all peoples will come to live together in a peace guaranteed by the binding force of mutual respect and love."

He also wrote, "In this final relationship, the Congress and the Administration have, on most vital issues, cooperated well, to serve the national good rather than mere partisanship, and so have assured that the business of the Nation should go forward. So, my official relationship with the Congress ends in a feeling, on my part, of gratitude that we have been able to do so much together."

Today we can hardly imagine such cooperation for the greater good of the American people. We would be foolishly in denial to believe there is no direct correlation between our wars and homelessness. Nor should we ignore the enormous percentage of US veterans who are bereft and discarded, living in poverty on the streets.

There was a time, not so long ago, in this country and others, those afflicted by poverty and hunger could come to a home in search of charity—a barn or back porch in which to sleep, a hot meal, kind words, and perhaps a day or two of work. Today most of us believe homeless people are nothing more than derelicts, alcoholics, and mentally unstable human debris.

The truth is quite different; the leading cause of homelessness is unaffordable shelter. The absence of jobs and low wages are other contributors to homelessness. Within the 'State of Homeless,' there is also a high rate of mental illness and alcoholism. Many of these contributing factors are treatable with better education, social services, and the availability of decent and affordable health care. The consequences of homelessness and anti-social behavior could be better prevented. In a way, it is an ongoing social conundrum. For thousands of families living on the edge, stress is a crippling factor disintegrating the bonds necessary for healthy family cohesion; studies have shown that stress alone can trigger the onset of devastating psychoses in children. Many men and women living on the streets today, diagnosed with mental illness, could have been treated at an early age and still could be.

We blame one another to such an extent that the concept of 'government' has become an alien and hostile separate entity. But ultimately, is there anyone to blame but us? A man who falls asleep at the wheel and crashes into a tree should not blame the car or the tree.

If the government is less or more than the common rulebook agreed upon by the majority, the pages sewn together by democratic principles to protect the commonality of all, we have failed. We have failed when millions of our children suffer hunger and poverty in a country as wealthy as the United States.

Rather than fighting foreign wars, which ultimately serve the already full coffers of the rich, our focus should be homelessness, poverty, and hunger in this country. Our most effective weapon is our voice and how we vote; we must fight for those who can't.

August 14, 2011

KADOS and ME
Journal Entries 2018-2022

In 2018, mulling over what to write in my forthcoming "The Journal," I again was visited by my other self, my alter-ego, some call it. I decided to go ahead and give him a name: Kados. I've long known, of course, that he's been with me, orbiting my existence, darting in at the last moment to keep me from making a fool of myself or even to save my life, or both, such as the time he guided my courage to jump off the diving board when I was five, or when he prevented me at age 13 from foolishly falling into the hands of a pedophile. I was grateful that he came to my rescue in 1984, insisting I release my non-functioning parachute, relying on faith and my emergency chute. He slips inside my mind efficiently, asking questions and offering advice or opinions but insisting more often than not.

OK. OK. I realize, Dear Reader, you might think I've been swimming in paint fumes too long; fifty years in the studio is a long time. Or you might believe Kados is nothing more than a writing ploy, something to entwine your imagination into mine. A little bit of both, I suspect. However, we're all blessed with some compelling, mysterious—perhaps even collective—voice that helps keep us on a more even keel. More balanced.

August 29, 2018

"Kados, I've been wondering about things I can't quite put my finger on. I suppose, in a way, because I've spent the last three years—damn near it—working on Sell The Monkey, a Memoir—autobiography, actually—I've neglected a part of my spirit that requires a different polish or poison or any number of different expressions we use to describe either one's addiction or ecstasy. I don't regret it, though. Not in the least."

"You shouldn't. Did you learn anything about yourself you didn't already know?"

"Not really. Well, that's not entirely true; I discovered things I'd never thought about precisely that way."

"Like what?"

"When you review what you've written so many times, looking for typos, wrong words used, words used too often, over-wrought or unnecessary expressions, split infinitives, being overly didactic or thinking something can be better said, or not said at all—then sure, you'll stumble over something from your past that finally makes sense as to what was happening then and possibly why it happened.

"Anyway, that's not what has captured my wonder. Now I find my appetite for visual creativity has set upon me with such clamor that I can hardly go through the day without dreaming of deep-diving into huge pots of paint. Acres of canvas, gessoed and stretched, roll across my visual dessert like sky dunes. Honestly, it seems…and yeah, I know what you'll say: "'Just dive in.'"

"So do it."

"Remember, Kados, I just turned seventy-four. You were here."

"You're concerned about age?"

"Of course. Age and pain, as you know, are grumpy roommates. Pain hurts. Frustrating as hell. One can't always do what one wants to do or should do. It's what it is; it comes with the clock."

"Indeed."

"But if you mean age in the sense of dying, of disappearing, no. As far as I can tell, Kados, we only disappear to those for whom we're dead. Beyond that…I can't be sure."

"Uh-huh. So, back to your point. What's your conundrum, if we can call it that?"

"It was over ten years ago when I decided my paintings should get smaller and smaller until they'd be no bigger than a butterfly's wing. I lied, of course. Big is in the works.

"Now that the book tour is over, I'm getting everything ready to submerge myself into an extended period of painting. Projections have begun; ideas flit about like glittering confetti. I'm halfway through converting my living space into a studio/workspace…again.

I have five months before blast off before I jettison into the mystery of my addiction. Painting. Process. Magic."

"What is it you're visualizing? Or have you gotten that far?"

"I think whatever appears will be about water, but I can't be sure. Part of the problem and, no doubt, the solution lies in the fact that I live by the river. I sleep and dream by the river. Its music has threaded me into its story so succinctly that I feel its joy and heartache in ways I can't explain. In the dreams, water's mystery lets me get only so close—I can almost touch it—then everything disappears, just around the bend."

"Then you understand."

"Understand what?"

"The simple and obvious truth that mystery is a mystery because it cannot be fathomed."

"I suppose, Kados, yes. And maybe it's the pull of mystery that keeps us searching. I want to believe so, anyway… I'd like to find…"

"Galen…"

"…to hold onto…"

"Galen…"

"What?"

"Let's go have lunch."

November 28, 2018

"What are you doing, Galen?"

"I'm writing—typing, to be exact—about what I hope to be doing."

"Yes, I see that, but why? Why write about it? Just do it."

"You don't understand, Kados. It's an alignment process."

"A what?"

"Never mind. You might remember that in late 2017, I decided I'd get back to painting. I promised Lennie I would. When I built my house here in the countryside of Northern Thailand, the open-air downstairs became my studio. It seemed perfect, but I soon realized the first floor wasn't high enough. Didn't work. I quickly built a high-roof shed on the side and began working on 'Notations. You remember? That series of paintings that…"

"Most of which you destroyed."

"Yeah, I know."

"But why? Why make something and then destroy it?"

"True. But the real problem, Kados, turned out to be the elements of the outside world—mildew, snails, frogs, lizards, wasps, ants, and mosquitos. They seemed to be my most excited patrons; they immediately began residing inside the stretchers, on the painted surface itself, basking in the color fields, building mud huts in the textured weave of the canvas, or leaving gloomy deposits of greyish white everywhere. Impossible.

"You do recall, Galen, why you left the United States. Remember the elephants?"

"Sure, of course."

'And do you recall what you told us when you left the commercial art world and your Seattle gallery?"

"Uh-huh."

"And surely you remember the little epigraphic poem you wrote not long ago."

"You mean the one about 'When I was young.'"

"Yeah, recite it."

"I can't remember it."

"Yes, you can. Say it with me. 'When I was young, I wanted to paint big. And I did. The older I get, the smaller I want to paint; today, a portrait the size of a postage stamp, tomorrow, a dream on the wing of a fly.'"

"So, what are you telling me, Kados? I can't change my mind."

"Galen, you're talking to your mind."

"Oh yeah, right."

"So why now? Why go back to these big canvases that are so damned enticing for insects and incredibly difficult to market? Why paint at all? You're old. Why don't you shuffle off to the garden and ruminate on 'what ifs,' 'whys,' and 'whens.'

"You're funny, Kados. In fact, I do. All the time. Have for years. Trying to figure out why I've made what I have, why more, and why me? Why is any of it important? Does it make a difference? Can it?"

"And?"

"And what?"

"Galen, have you figured anything out?"

"No. Truthfully, friend, there's no answer to such questions. I can only say that when the gods set us down for this short stay, they gave us something to bind us one to another, to remember those who came before, and possibly to help those who follow. I want to believe so. We've shaped poems, told stories, painted paintings, and made music for as long as—no, longer than—the gods have shadowed us. Art is this ineffable ocean of human expression made for and despite ourselves; it is a fingerprint of our history. Do you not believe, Kados, that anything so long-lasting has a reason and a purpose for its durability?

"I don't know, Galen, but I feel like I'm drifting into a poor man's Socratic dialogue. Talk about here and now and why."

"OK. The new studio space that was my main living space, upstairs and fully enclosed, protected from the elements, is nearly done. I've designed it to hold anywhere from eight to ten paintings in progress that can be rolled and stored for shipping. I plan to create a series of large paintings, perhaps 15 to 20 in all, of various sizes, but on average, roughly about 6' x 7,' some larger, some smaller, over the next 12 to 18 months. I plan on returning, in part, to visual explorations I made in the late 1970s, juxtaposing shapes that dance, shift, and realign across the picture plane, creating a rhythm, if you will, Kados, of visual tensions and resolutions."

"Just do it, Galen. Do it.'"

December 16, 2018

The winter sky is spooling out a pale Vermeer blue. It gently spreads through the woods and across the rice fields while I sit gazing out of my large window, watching these lovely old trees catch the light and feed it to the nearby river. Summer rains have been generous.

I alternately contemplate between the landscape before me and bursts of image ideas from within. I try to freeze them in my mind. How will they get through me into reality? What paths are taken? This part is never easy, not because I've lost my way but because there are so many paths, so many ideas to choose from, and the older I get, new possibilities indiscriminately weave into those of a lifetime, never fully resolved, merely evolving into yet another reflection. Still, as I observe the morning light spin across the water, I begin to stitch together a new visual language and how it might take shape as part of this luminous miracle life has given me. I've grown old in this wrinkled sheath of skin, blessed by being loved, loving, and remembering love. Knowing where I am and processing what is and what isn't, what works, and what doesn't, is a blessing I hold onto.

Last July, When I turned seventy-four, I not so seriously calculated how much of my life I've devoted to making art. All of it? In some ways, yes, of course; there is that curious little itch encrypted in the genes of my DNA blueprint. When I made the commitment to make art slightly over forty-five years ago, I'd venture to say the arc of my creative processing, which can occur in every gear of the mind at any time—reading, eating, sleeping, biological functions, and all social synapses—has occupied a good chunk of my life's clock. Though I'm not an obsessive artist nor particularly prolific, I can confidently estimate I've turned over the same ruminations during at least a third of my time on earth. Imagine: forty-seven quadrillion nanoseconds fishing in the unknown, then serving up the results in one expression or another. Why? Why, indeed. There's no way to measure why any one person makes art or the results from doing so. Nothing other than belief.

As I knew they would, the images began speaking to me, blooming into my consciousness, growing hungrier, more precise, zigzagging across the busy streets of my occipital lobe, spilling out into the morning light, struggling for definition, insisting themselves to a fully charged input, ready to be made whole.

I'm delighted but ever cautious. Every act of painting is a dance with uncertainty; I know this all too well.

"Be patient," I tell them.

"Simplicity," they demand.

"OK. I like that." I offer.

"Give us color, rich and pure, the kind of hues the mind adores. And contrast the shapes, if you would, and shift them, so the language is clear."

"Anything else?" I ask.

"Yes. One more thing."

"What is it?"

"Keep us close to your breathing, to your heartbeat."

"I will," I answer, smiling, moving away from the window back to the studio.

March 2019

Like most days, I wake early this morning from the plaintive cry of the Asian Koel, Eudynamys scolopaceus. It's impossible not to. The Koel, a member of the Cuckoo family, has the loudest mating call in all of Thailand. My feathered alarm clock is black, with a hooked beak and crimson eyes, about 18 inches long, and begins its morning perched in the mango tree that grows beside my bedroom. His mating call is piercing and cadenced, sounding very much like 'For real, for real, for real,' alerting me, no doubt, that Dreamtime is over; the day begins for real.

I sit on the edge of the bed, slow-stretching out coils of sleep. Lately, in these unusual days of isolation, I've begun a morning ritual, celebrating each day with a mantra of gratitude: Thank you, dear body, for caring for me, bringing me through this long river of time, unfolding into the present, precious moment. A confluence of bones, muscles, tendons, and ligaments keeps me upright and mobile; beautiful winged ribs cradle my heart, protecting these breathing lungs. I bow to the metabolic machinery, the factories of chemicals and minerals, to legions of soldiers who do their best to ward off invaders. Oh, praise to you, beautiful blood, captain of this ship, magnificent and sacred water coursing through every fiber, delivering to and taking away what the body needs or doesn't need. Sea of my potential, feed these thoughts I carry with goodness, hold my memories equally sacred, and let me ascend into the ether, touching everything all at once.

I then rise into early morning patterns, herding my daily questions out of the corral where I'd left them the night before. Do I begin painting today? Do I finish this journal or repair the leak in my roof? Is there time for the world to start again?

I make coffee and nod a greeting to one of a handful of geckos with whom I share my tiny house. Interestingly and gratefully, their population remains consistent; only a dozen reside throughout the rooms, living and hunting primarily on the ceiling, darting behind my paintings on the walls when I move too close. We tolerate each other in quiet reciprocity. They're proficient at catching insects that are adept at dining on me.

I walk outside, across the porch, and down the garden stairs. My eyes catch a faint movement–a reflection coming from within the pond. I lean closer and discover a few water droplets have settled onto the veins of the lotus leaf, each crystal orb spinning out a universe of light. I bend closer to inspect one drop that appears unusually different from the others–an encapsulating movement I know too well.

"Is that you, Kados?

"Of course, it's me."

"What are you doing?"

"The same as you. Contemplating. Ruminating. Or should we call it 'Fabulating?'"

"Yeah. I like that. Why not?"

Indeed, why not? After all, Galen, we've become searchers in these star-lit sands, scratching for clues beneath the surface of our desert. Now we must burrow into these dunes and wait with patience. Hopefully, some infant energy will descend and light us a way out."

June 2019

Kados and I've been busy in the studio, turning visual somersaults, lassoing in a herd of ideas enough to at least have them feel as if they're born of the same symphony. I do the dirty work, of course—building the frame, stretching the canvas, mixing the paint, scrubbing and scumbling the surface, cleaning up afterward—while

Kados opines from his lofty interior perch as to whether all this energy flow holds a measure of value that I hope it does or even, often enough, any at all.

"I think we have something," he'll proclaim when, after much fretting and uncertainty from my side, a painting boldly asserts itself as if I had nothing to do with its successful birth. Or just as likely, as he did today, he'll say, "Sorry, Galen, but what you've found feels as dense as a cupful of mud. Better scrub it out and re-approach…with less 'you' this time. You know what I mean, right?"

I do know what he means; I can't deny it. Kados, my beloved shadow, has a perspective I don't have; he's more intuitive and targeted. I concede.

"Thanks, Kados. I appreciate your guidance, brutal as it often is. I'm grateful. I don't know what I'd do without you."

"You couldn't," he mumbled, alternately appearing and disappearing within the pulsing of our heart.

I've often wondered, since having given my alter ego a name, if Kados is nothing more than the opposite side of this self I think of as me, as if on one side of a blank sheet of paper, facing me, is written the name Galen and on the other side is written Kados, facing everything I cannot see. Is this how we came into being? Or was Kados already here as I was squeezed out of a dark nothing into the light of everything? I don't know. And if Kados knows, he's not saying.

"You could be a bit more helpful, Kados."

"What is it you need?"

"Here it is. Slightly over two years ago, past images—meditative and dreamlike—revisited, reeling me back into their dominion, having first appeared as the Pneuma Shift Series four decades ago, then suddenly disappeared that same year, 1982, when I tried to conjure them back. Gone. Nowhere to be found. OK. OK. I know it sometimes takes a while to complete a vision. So when they returned in 2018, I welcomed them back; A journey complete, I told myself. But no, they persist. Relentlessly, it seems.

"So?"

"Have I no control, Kados? No say-so in the matter? I keep thinking that I need to be, should be, or want to be exploding great bombs of color in wild abstractions, rioting across the canvas like a monkey on LSD. I dream of it, then the next day, as I contemplate the physical dive, the shadow of Pneuma Shift slips in, wedges herself between me…or us, I should say…and the Big Bang, as it were. Then all is lost. Or is it? I'm confused."

"Have patience, Galen. Surely there's a reason for these long, persistent 'escapes' to unwind as they do, as they must. Think of it as the quiet before the storm, the ending of the beginning. Be grateful for where this light takes you. Time to drift beneath the covers of sleep, I think. Tomorrow. Tomorrow. Tomorrow."

November 2019

In a previous Journal entry, when I queried Kados about "what now?" my inimitable second self replied, "Have patience, brother."

OK. I quietly suspended the painting for a while and have begun to focus on a campaign to get NOSTOS, the most recent painting series, framed and shipped back to the United States, as well as getting my current book project, BENCH, A Story of Wonder, launched into the world, and, of course, myself back to the country of my birth to promote the book, its message, and finding homes for the paintings. It's all part of the same brush stroke.

Unfortunately, the world is still wobbling from being slapped by the pandemic. Much more than its usual teeter. I'd hoped to get back this month a year ago, avoiding the seasonal pollution that seems worse each year in Northern Thailand, but because travel is impossible, hunkering down, I believe it's called, is where we are. If I can get vaccinated against COVID by early June, I'll launch a travel campaign to get me back by August or September. If not, a reset for March of 2022 will fall into play.

"Here we are, Kados, spiraling toward our 77th year—you, me, our many friends, that old cat S̄ī k̄hāw sleeping all day long, the fish in the river joyfully chasing water's dancing light, all the trees, and their trembling leaves—bending into the winds of time. And waiting for what? A reversal?

"May I ask you the difference between 'was' and 'will be,' or is it always only 'now?' Seventy-seven years? Damn! Still, by any measurement, being here is a joyful miracle, no matter how many aggravating obstacles we face or which time dimension we embrace."

"Yes, I know, Galen. It absolutely is. And think of it. We're only a faint whisper fading into silence; even I, your invisible other-self, often feel this tugging urge to let go and start over. But all of us— you and me, your friends, the lazy cat, the rafting fish, the trembling heart's hunger for light—spiral endlessly into this loving moment again and again." Do you feel it?

"No. feel what?"

"The numbers, Galen. You were born on July 7, 1944."

"So?"

"They're such an auspicious set of numbers. You're seventy-seven years old, born 7/7/44.

"You mean 'we' are, but go on."

The number 7 puts you between the world of the living and the dying, a balance toward completeness. 77 minus 44 = 33; this is Trāyastriṃśa, a word that arrives from the number 33, symbolizing the second in the six heavens of the Buddhist cosmological desire realm. And don't forget: 33 is the sum of three cubes. Oh, and there's this iteration: 4 plus 4 = 8, minus 1 = 7 or 4th primary number, 7 minus 4 = 3, the 2nd primary number; 3 minus 2 leaves you with number 1, this journey for a new beginning."

"Uh-huh. Is this it, Kados? I turned back toward the house, looking for my cat. "So, if this is it, what is this that is, and why is that?"

A long silence unspools, then Kados and I fall off the bench, tossing and tumbling into a cloud of dying leaves, laughing uncontrollably, our tears streaming into the river. At this point, I pull myself together, back into me—not Kados, just me—sitting by the river, trying to meditate on being one with the cosmos. Still, I hear myself ask, "What's so funny, Kados?"

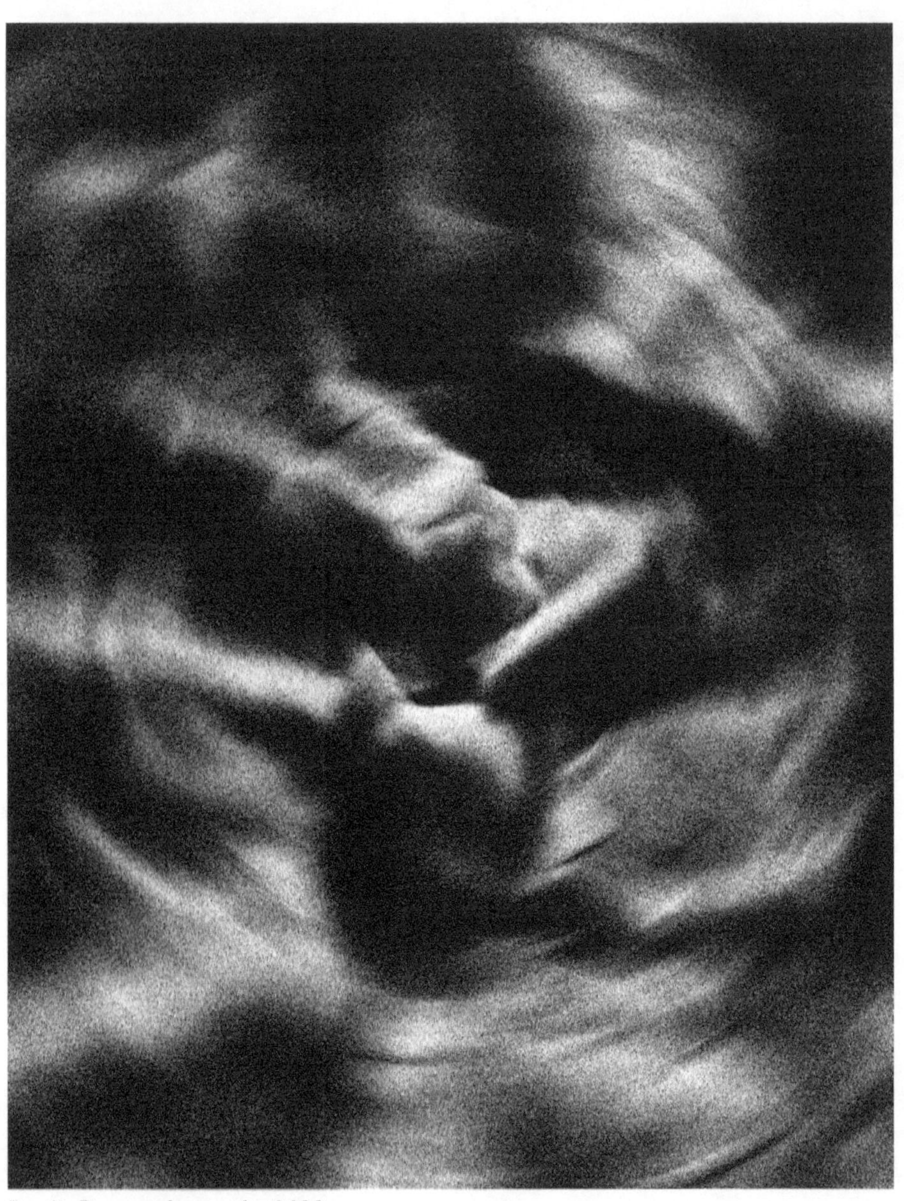

Rumi's Dance, galenograph, 2022

"You are, dear boy. You have this tilted belief that I, Kados, am your second self, your alter-ego, your lover in battle, your imperturbable mischief, when, in fact, I am none of these."

"Impossible, Kados. You're my invention; I gave you your name. Are we not the same bit of breath? The same heartbeat? If you're not me, not mine, then who are you?

"You'll know at the journey's end, dear friend. Have patience."

"So what do we do now, Kados? Where do we go from here?"

"Let's feed the cat…then go dancing with the wind."